THE STOKER

THE STOKER

TEN YEARS FIGHTING RED AGGRESSION AND OTHER
SOCIAL DISEASES IN THE SERVICE OF ONE'S COUNTRY

A MEMOIR

L. MEL MCCONAGHY

[N₁ [O₂ [N₁

CANADA

Library and Archives Canada Cataloguing in Publication

McConaghy, L. Mel, 1936–

The stoker : ten years fighting red aggression and other social diseases in
the service of one's country : a memoir / L. Mel McConaghy.

ISBN 978–0–9739558–6–6

1. McConaghy, L. Mel, 1936–.

2. Cold War.

3. Canada—History, Military.

4. Canada. Royal Canadian Navy—Biography.

5. Great Britain. Royal Navy—Biography.

6. Sailors—Canada—Biography.

I. Title.

V64.C32M33 2009   359.0092   C2009–905379–9

Printed and bound in Canada on 100% ancient forest-free paper.

Now Or Never Publishing
11268 Dawson Place
Delta, British Columbia
Canada V4C 3S7

nonpublishing.com
Fighting Words.

I would like to dedicate this book to my wife Barbara, our kids and my family for the love and support they have given me. Without them I would be a rudderless ship floundering on the sea of life.

Forthwith this frame of mine was wrenched
With a woeful agony,
Which forced me to begin my tale;
And then it left me free.

~ Samuel Taylor Coleridge, *The Rime of the Ancient Mariner*

I

It was late summer, the year 1954, and not only had our logging foreman told us it was time to shut down for the season, but Mother Nature was starting to give us subtle hints as well. The days were getting shorter and the leaves were starting to turn, offering us a last blast of autumn colour before the winter's grey set in. We wouldn't be working in the bush again until the muskeg froze and ice settled on the lake.

One night not long afterwards I was at a party with my old buddy Skip Robbins. We had our pockets full of money after having earned a whopping $1.25 an hour all summer, which probably meant around $400 between the two of us. Someone asked Skip, "What are you two clowns going to do until we start up again?"

"Oh I dunno," slurred Skip in his rapidly advancing state of intoxication. "Maybe we'll go and join the navy." This statement brought a round of laughter, as well it should have, considering who it might be doing the joining.

"I doubt the navy is that hard up for men that they'd take the pair of you," came the expected reply.

"Oh yeah? Well betcha, what, ten dollars they'd be happy to have a couple of able-bodied men like us—right, Mel?"

The sound of my name and the mention of ten dollars took me away, momentarily, from my pursuit of a young lady who, at that point of the night, looked an awful lot like Marilyn Monroe when, in actual fact, in the cruel light of day and without the benefit of the alcohol's rosy mist and the bad lighting, she had dark hair and was built more like a mason jar than an hourglass.

"You betcha, Skip—whatever," I said. Not surprisingly, Skip and I agreed on just about everything, especially at a party. We'd been working and hanging around together for over a year now, and had built up a pretty good friendship as a result. He was a likeable guy, about 5–foot–10 with a stocky build; he had a great head of sandy curly hair roofing a round face, and a slightly turned up nose with just a hint of freckles. He was an easy person to like with his impish grin and matching sense of humour and girls, especially older women, seemed to love running their fingers through his hair. In retrospect, I think they wanted to mother him. I don't remember what his real first name was— Harry James or something like that—I think when he was born his mother had a crush on some famous big band leader at the time—but he was Skip to everyone else.

Skip didn't really give a damn what people thought of him and would say just about anything that came to mind while I, on the other hand, happened to be very self-conscious and thus none too outspoken at the time. When I think back, we had to be about the two most contradictory personalities you could ever run into together, but maybe that's why we got along so well.

Skip and I did have one thing in common though: we both liked girls. The only difference was, I would fall in love while Skip would fall in lust. I was a romantic; Skip was more of a horny clown. I would always get a nice goodnight kiss; Skip would get laid. I would be considered a gentleman; Skip would get laid. At this time of my life, a girl I thought I was in love with, the girl I'd wanted to spend the rest of my life with, had just dumped me, which left me even more gun-shy. Even so, in the matter and manner of women, Skip was a lot smarter than I.

We didn't have a Foreign Legion, so why not the navy, we thought. After all, if you're going to run away, you might just as well run away on a boat; sailing's a lot easier than marching. We could have joined the air force right there in Prince George, but after much deliberation, about fifteen seconds or so, we decided the sailors' suits would be that much more appealing to the girls. The next ten years of my life were to be based on this single assessment.

We hung around Prince George for a week or two, but with the taunting of our so-called friends and the idea of having to pay someone ten dollars, we bid our mothers and siblings goodbye and headed for the coast. After a short expensive stopover in Vancouver to give the girls there the gift of our presence and a great deal of our money, we caught the ferry to Victoria. Besides, we weren't going to need money; the navy was going to take care of us. Or so we thought.

Joining the navy turned out to be more complicated than we had initially anticipated. They wanted to know this and that and they wanted documentation for all of it. The fact I had a grade eight education was suddenly a little difficult to prove. I had come by it in a roundabout way. When I was fourteen years old, I was going to Prince George Junior-Senior High School. I was about halfway through grade eight and doing quite well. The only problem was, according to my teachers, I was mentally lazy (in those days if you were dyslexic you were either mentally lazy or stupid) and would sooner be riding in a lumber truck than sitting in a classroom.

One day our Principal, Mister Ray Williston, called me into his office and said, "Lester,"—that's my actual first name—"you are not doing yourself or me any good by being here. I think it's time you go out and pursue whatever it is you want to do with your life."

So I left school.

Now before you go thinking that such a statement by a person in his position seemed a little harsh, it is important to realize that Mister Williston was a very intelligent man. After his stint as Principal, he later became the Minister of Forests for the government at the time. Williston Lake was named after him.

Then, early in my working career, I ruptured my appendix. While I was busy convulsing, the teacher of the small one-room school in the little mill town of Aleza Lake in which I lived, some 45 miles east of Prince George, formulated a plan. Every spring the schools from all the mill towns along the East Line, as the railroad running east out off Prince George was very astutely called at the time, put on a track meet, and a trophy was awarded to the school with the most points. As it was, our Aleza Lake School was one of the smallest, with the least amount of students, and it never won.

Most of the twelve students were younger and had to compete against older and bigger students from the other schools, and they were always missing out on the first place medals. Well this teacher wanted to change all that. He was a very enterprising young man. So we made a deal. He would get me my grade eight diploma if I, being a fairly good athlete, would compete at the track meet for his school that spring.

My school days were usually a pretty laid back affair. After the teacher gave the rest of the students their assignments, he and I would go sit on the front porch and smoke a cigarette, and talk about girls and the other really important things in life. Then it was a matter of completing a couple of small assignments before heading home. This was a lot better then the regimentation of Mr. Williston's School, I clearly remember thinking at the time.

The track meet was a success. I won three or four firsts and a couple of seconds, and with the formula they used based on student population, little Aleza Lake won the trophy.

There was a lot of talk about our school bringing in a ringer, so I finished grade eight in order to make it legitimate. I wasn't given any sort of actual certificate, but I was assured it was on record. But now it was creating a holdup in our application process, finding this record.

And so we waited. And waited. And every day I phoned the recruiting office to find out what was happening. "Not all the documentation has come through yet. They're having trouble finding your school records," was the answer I got.

By this time we'd moved into a little motel in Esquimalt where a lot of old age pensioners lived. It was quite a bit cheaper than the hotel room we'd been living in and besides, our summer money was rapidly running out. The room had two single beds, a table, two chairs, a hot plate and a small refrigerator, and the landlady had given us a couple of plates, utensils and some pots and pans so we could cook for ourselves. It wasn't palatial, but at least it was affordable.

As it was, there was a little restaurant about a block from the motel, and the lady who owned it took a liking to us, or maybe just to Skip. When she learned of our plight, she had us wash dishes and perform other odd jobs around the place, and in return she fed us three squares a day.

About this time we were considering hitchhiking home, and that would have been no easy task considering we were on an island. Then suddenly I got the call to report to the recruiting office to pick up my travel warrant, tickets and meal vouchers. I was on my way. I was officially in the navy. Skip, however, wouldn't be leaving until the following week, which concerned me a little bit.

The lady at the restaurant had a little going-away party for me, though it seemed to me that both she and Skip were a little too happy to see me leave. Being buddies, I offered him part of the money I had left, but he assured me he'd be all right. I often wondered if maybe I'd been getting in the way of his carnal endeavours. In retrospect we were being fed pretty well for doing so little work around the place.

2

On the 21st of September 1954 I officially became a member of the Royal Canadian Navy. Ordinary Seaman Engineering Mechanic, Lester Melvin McConaghy, official number 18464–E. At the time I recall questioning this title, "Ordinary Seaman" because, to be honest, I was feeling pretty damned special.

Special or not, they shipped me off to Vancouver on the ferry in order to catch the train that was to take me across Canada to HMCS Cornwallis in Nova Scotia. I remember strutting around that old CPR ferry like a worldly man of the sea, when in actual fact I was just a kid from Aleza Lake who suddenly found himself on salt water for the second time in his life.

Without a uniform no one onboard seemed to have any idea I was a sailor, and every time I ran into someone in uniform I would nod knowingly and greet them enthusiastically. Sometimes they returned my greeting, but most of the time they simply ignored me. Somehow they couldn't tell by my seagoing swagger that I, too, was a man of the sea. In reality, I was shy to the point that, at an earlier age, I would stutter when I talked to more than one person at a time, unless I was in the company of a friend. Skip had a way of bringing me out of my shell.

When I was younger I was very insecure and a bit of a loner, and enjoyed the fantasyland of the movies. I had a very vivid imagination, and often preferred my imaginary friends to some of the real ones I had. This all stemmed from the fact my mother was widowed, the first time, when I was nine months old, leaving her with two older girls, my brother and me. Then she was widowed again when I was around twelve, leaving her with an additional three sons and the burden of raising seven of us kids on her own.

Life was tough for my mother. A navy shrink told me, later in my career, that this gave me a sense of insecurity and low self-esteem. "Is that so," I told her. "And all this time I've been thinking I'm a fairly well adjusted young man." I think this was the same shrink who asked me how old I was when I first had sex. "Oh I guess I was twelve or thirteen," I said.

"My god," she gasped. "How old was your partner?"

"Oh I never had a partner until I was around seventeen." The interview was terminated at this point, as I recall. I think I was starting to come out of my shell, and a lot of the things I'd wished I'd said over the years I was starting to say.

However, I will admit I was feeling a little insecure when we docked in Vancouver and a navy car whisked me off to catch the train.

You can imagine the excitement I was trying to suppress, what with this great adventure I was about to embark upon. To this point, the farthest I'd travelled by train was the 45–mile ride from Prince George to Aleza Lake, and here I was about to cross the entire country on one.

I had fantasized about it when I was a few years younger, standing there on the station platform at Aleza Lake when the passenger train pulled in to drop off the people returning from Prince George. This was what you did in a small mill community for excitement, when you only had your radio to listen to or your neighbours to visit for coffee or play softball with in the summer.

I remember gazing with great envy at the people in the windows of the train when it pulled in every Tuesday, Thursday and Saturday evening, before rocketing its way east to places I'd only heard about from some worldly traveller or read about in the National Geographic Magazine. I remember seeing them lounging in the comfort of the passenger coach or in the luxury of the dining car, looking down at this kid from some nondescript whistle stop with expressions of what could only be described as indifference. I could imagine them thinking, "A nobody from nowhere, going no place." So when I boarded the sleeper car that day in Vancouver, I was thinking of telling these people, "Hey, have a look now. Look who's going some place." It was a quiet moment of vindication for me.

I was quite surprised to find there were six more recruits going with me. I also learned we'd be picking up more at every major stop along the way. I had thought, in my ignorance, that maybe there would only be a select few of us picked for this wonderful adventure, not a whole damned mob like there turned out to be.

I also learned that all of us weren't the cream of the Canadian crop, as it were. Some of these guys were pretty tough characters that some benevolent judge or magistrate had given the choice, "Either join the service or go to jail." But these were not hardened criminals. They were only rambunctious young men who'd strayed a little outside society's strict boundaries and been caught.

Every week a new division of recruits started their training at HMCS Cornwallis, located just outside the little maritime town of Digby, Nova Scotia, and every week a trainload of young recruits just like ours would make the journey across Canada, some from small towns, others from cities, some from farms and others from right out of the bush, but all with their own reasons for joining the navy and all with their own distinct personalities.

The conductors and porters were wise to us, and to what to expect from us. Mothers didn't let their teenaged daughters wander too far from their sides. Older people frowned, and looked down their noses at us, and when they found out we were navy recruits, shook their heads in utter disbelief, mumbling things like, "What's this country coming to when they enlist hooligans like this to protect us." It seems to me it's always been thus.

Some of the guys had known others who'd already gone through basic training, and were eagerly repeating tales told about it. The refrain most often repeated was, "You'll be sorry." These words we were to hear over and over again, mostly from the old salts who'd been at Cornwallis for all of a week or more.

We rattled across Canada. At every major stop along the line our numbers increased, so that by the time we reached Montreal there was a whole gang of us onboard. This motley crew, plus the rest of the recruits from eastern Canada, were to make up the

Nootka 7 division for the next four months in HMCS Cornwallis. The previous Nootka Division, Nootka 6, had passed out, or graduated, from basic training the Friday we arrived. Each division, named after a ship from World War I or II, was comprised of about sixty bodies, a "body" being the term the navy used in reference to its recruits. This was all right, I surmised, as long as they were still warm bodies by the end of it.

3

The morning the buses unloaded us at the base—everything from farm boys in their Sunday best to zoot-suiters with baggy pants and ducktail haircuts—it was quite a culture shock.

Before we had left our various departure points, we'd been told to leave most of our civilian clothes at home, because we wouldn't be needing them the next four months. Except for what I was wearing, and a couple of extra shorts and shocks, I had dutifully complied and sent most of mine back to Aleza Lake. Well you can imagine what some of us looked and smelled like after a week on the train without benefit of showers and only a sponge bath in one of those tiny onboard sinks.

As we came off the bus chattering and laughing like a bunch of schoolgirls, we were met by what seemed the meanest, nastiest men imaginable. They were hollering at us at the top of their collective lungs, all at the same time, from every angle:

"Fall in columns of three, dress by the right, you bunch of idiots!

"Shut those gobs! Where the hell do you think you are, at a church social?

"Move lively! Straighten up those shoulders! You look like a bunch of little old ladies!

"Get in line, columns of three. I said *three*! Can't you count, you bunch of clowns?"

The sheer volume and ferocity of their voices had us milling about like a herd of sheep surrounded by a pack of wolves, when in actual fact there were but five of them and scores of us. Still, you knew immediately who the wolves were by their treatment of the sheep, and in charge was the worst wolf of all.

On the parade square, the Gunnery Chief was God. His boots shone to a high gloss that made a showroom car look pallid, his uniform was equally immaculate, and even though he appeared to be a man well into his forties, he always stood ramrod straight. Over the next few months I would witness this impressive figure giving new officers close order drill on the parade square, hollering in his booming voice such helpful hints as, "I said your left foot, you clumsy idiot, *sir.*" Exercising his well-earned authority, he employed only the minimum amount of respect for the fledgling officer's rank.

His two leading seamen were equally as impressive—ramrod straight, arms pulled straight down at their sides, fist clenched at the first knuckle, palms turned in and thumbs pointed to the ground—just like they would drum into our heads for countless hours on the parade square over the next four months. They wore the Round Rig most everyone associates with a sailor, a tight-fitting jumper with a wide blue collar faded from many washings, and bellbottom pants tucked smartly into white gators (the army calls them putties). The Round Rig was the sign of an old salt, a man of many voyages and a veteran of the sea, and these two were the epitome of the sailor and the silent envy of all the recruits in the Nootka 7 division that day and for many days to come.

These two turned out to be our Divisional Officer and Chief Petty Officer. The Divisional Officer was Lieutenant Walker, a smart looking individual in his early- to mid-thirties, with a head of blonde hair pushing out from under his officer's cap, a soft angular face, and a hawk-like nose. His bearing demanded respect, and his soft blue eyes gave the impression that he was a man you could trust, as was the case with Chief Petty Officer Beamish, our Divisional Chief, a short round man with an equally round face reminiscent of someone's grandfather. These two men would be, for the next four months, our mentors and guardians. They would be our guides into this wider world we had chosen to enter, a world of travel and of discipline. A world where, though you might dislike a person, you would willingly trust him with your life, because you knew he was a professional.

The next few days weny by in a blur. First, we were marched down to the barbershop at the double to receive our first dreadful haircuts. (I had the impression these so-called barbers weren't really barbers at all, but merely people from the street eager to cut hair for a laugh.) In fact, we went everywhere at the double, which meant we jogged in step for the entire four months of basic training, except for the final week when we marched with the pride of a division in its waning days of basic training, and on Sundays for church parade. After our haircuts, we were double marched up to the clothing stores to receive our kit, in it everything we would need for our next five years of navy life.

We lined up at the clothing stores in alphabetical order, just like we would line up for the next five years of our lives, for everything in the navy, including one's pay, came at the end of a very long line.

The clothing stores had a long counter with shelves full of gear on one side and the whole lot of us on the other. I really believe it was a game with these people working here, seeing how fast they could kit out a division of sixty men. They were very good at this game and knew it, and wanted each of us to know it too.

It seemed to me, at this point of my naval career, that we recruits were the only ones happy to be here. No one seemed to smile, and if you did, someone would immediately shout at you, "Wipe that smile of your face, sailor." At least they were calling us sailors.

There was no trying on clothes for fit, just, "What's your waist size?"

"Thirty-two inches, and I have a thirty-inch inseam."

"Did I ask you for your inseam?"

"No."

"No, sir."

"Yes, sir. No, sir."

At this point I was just beginning to learn that with everything that walked, talked or breathed it was best to begin all requests and answer all questions with "sir." And if it had gold on its hat, salute it. Salute the hell out of it in fact.

We went through the line-up at almost a run.

"Shoe size?"

'Oh my god, what's my shoe size,' I thought as the panic set in. "Nine and a half, I think, sir."

"Well if they aren't now, they soon will be, sailor," the man said, handing me two pair of boots and a pair of shoes.

Boots, shoes, shorts, hair brush, tooth brush, shoe brushes, socks, two white summer hats, one black winter hat, work clothes and, oh yes, a round tin hat box and kit bag to carry all your worldly possessions including three serge uniforms, a number one and two number twos, the difference being the number one had gold badges on the shoulders and the number two had red ones, all of which we were to sew on ourselves. Also included were two white tropical uniforms I don't think I wore until I served on the Royal Yacht five years later. Then it was off to the kit marking building where we labelled everything with our names and serial numbers with needle and thread. We even had to label our tin hat box with steel wool, or so some smart ass Leading Hand informed us. We had to call him sir too. This was one time in my life I almost hated my name, with all its letters.

In the mornings we made up our bunks to ridiculously strict specifications. And having made them, we then watched the Leading Hand drop a quarter on them. "That quarter didn't bounce. Tear it apart and make it properly, McCo—McCona—whatever the hell your name is. I'll have my eye on you." Everyone had their eye on you. And ten years later I still had people stumbling over my name. Whenever I thought it was a problem, or they were, I would let them stumble. It made them lose some of their holier than thou attitude.

They always made a point of picking some baby-faced kid.

"Did you shave this morning, sailor?"

"No, sir. I don't shave yet, sir."

"What do you mean you *don't shave yet*? It states in the Queen's Rules and Regulations that you shall shave every morning, so I don't want to hear you say you didn't shave!" By this time the officer was standing right up against the kid, hollering in his face, and you had to know what the kid was thinking.

We learned how to march for hours upon hours, pounding around the parade square with the ever-present drill instructors screaming at the tops of their lungs. I don't think there has ever been a person who, while learning to march, when given the order to "quick march," hasn't started out swinging their right arm ahead at the same time as their right foot. Well this poor bastard, stumbling along in parade formation, trying to get his arms and legs back in sync and in step with everyone else, always incurred the wrath of the instructors. "I said left, you half wit. Don't you know your left from your right? Maybe we should put some hay in your left boot and straw in the right and call out 'hay foot, straw foot' and then maybe, just maybe, you bunch of plough jockeys will get it right."

When I think back now, I realize these people were very creative in coming up with ways to call us stupid. But we did learn discipline, we did learn how to march, and perhaps most importantly, we did learn our left foot from our right.

Each division had its own building, or "block" as it was called. The division was split into four watches. There was a port watch and a starboard watch, each of which was divided into two more watches, first and second, so you had a first of port watch and a second of port watch. The starboard watch was divided up the same way. This system was uniform throughout the navy.

The block was a long, two-storey building with an entrance at one end and stairs and washrooms at the other. In between was a long room with bunks on either side. Every second bunk had a little wall separating it from the next, which formed what was called a "cubicle." There were two sailors assigned to each cubicle, and I shared mine with a tall, raw-boned kid from Newfoundland by the name of John Brenton. John, with his "Newfy" accent and easy sense of humour, made the time I spent there almost a pleasure. This great, gangly man turned out to be just about the toughest bastard I ever met, and definitely one of the most pleasant, a rare combination if ever there was one.

The bottom floor was allotted to the port watch, the front half to the first of port watch and back half to the second of port watch, while the top floor was split up the same way for the starboard watch. We had no maids or janitor service, so the division was responsible for the block—we cleaned it to a spotless shine time and time again. At any time of day or night, the powers that be could come parading in for one of their little inspections, and you were at the mercy of just about anyone or anything that outranked you. As the drill instructors were fond of telling us, "The whole damned division could march under a snake's belly standing upright, that's how low you are."

The first week went charging by, just like the train that had brought us here. They checked us out at the dental clinic, my first encounter with the army dentists or "jawbreakers" as most everyone referred to them. I think the army must have sent their trainees to Cornwallis to give them some experience, because they certainly didn't seem to have any experience coming in.

Then it was off to the medical clinic, or "sickbay" in navy terms, to be poked, prodded and held while you turned your head to the right and coughed. They stuck things in your ears and in your mouth while you said, "Ahh," checking for this and that and God knows what else. Then they sent you to the shrink to be "evaluated." This, in my mind, was the fun part. After all, these were some awfully intelligent and serious people that seemed intent on asking some awfully stupid questions. It was a treat to watch their expressions when you came up with a really good answer.

To my surprise, I was issued eyeglasses. Here I'd been wandering around the first eighteen years of my life not realizing I really couldn't see that well. But when they issued me my first pair of glasses there at Cornwallis, it was like someone opened up a whole new world to me. I suddenly realized why, in my younger years, I kept getting hit by the softball instead of catching it. Convinced for so long that I was just a lousy ball player, it was in fact because I had such lousy eyesight.

On Friday, the new division arrived, including good old Skip. Now it was Nootka 7's turn to holler, "You'll be sorry," and we didn't disappoint. Every Friday afternoon, each division got dressed up in their number one uniforms for what was called "Divisions," a parade in which everyone marched around and watched the graduating division pass out of basic training. The following Friday would be Skip's first Divisions, in which they would assume the name Gatineau, the name of the division passing out that day. This ritual was carried out every Friday afternoon, rain or shine, summer and winter, either out on the parade square or in the massive drill hall, for as long as HMCS Cornwallis was a training base.

You stood there at attention, watching as your division's name moved up one more space on the big board that looked like a ladder on the side of the drill shed, and the name of the passing-out division plunged to the bottom only to start its slow, relentless crawl to the top again. One week, two weeks, three weeks—great, we only have thirteen weeks to go until we are unleashed from this self-imposed prison of repetition and discipline upon the daughters of a poor unsuspecting Canadian public.

For fifteen weeks you went everywhere at the double: you ran to breakfast and you ran to dinner and in between you ran to the parade square where you learned to run some more. You learned to tie knots in ropes, you learned the difference between a ship and a boat, and you learned that the pointy end was the stem or bow and the square end was the stern. You learned that floors were decks, that ceilings were deck heads and that everything attached to them were on the overhead, and that the walls were bulkheads. But mostly you learned your kit. Your kit had to be rolled and tied in little bundles exactly eight inches long with your name and official number showing, and if they called for a "kit muster" you had to lay it out on your bunk in just the prescribed way, in just the prescribed place. The only things that weren't rolled and tied in little round bundles on the bunk were the clothes you were wearing that day. You soon learned the only things that were ever unrolled were the clothes you would need the next day, and you learned to wash everything as you finished wearing it, that very night. This saved having to roll it all up again.

I believe it was around our tenth week of basic training when we finally went to sea.

One cold wet winter's morning we packed up what gear we'd need for the five days we were going to spend on the

HMCS Buckingham that had, sometime during the previous night, slipped in alongside the jetty at Cornwallis.

With a great deal of excitement, and all our gear, we marched at the double down to the ship. A lot of the guys had never seen a ship, let alone been aboard one, especially the guys from the Prairies, but I had the benefit of having seen ships on my short visit to Victoria and Vancouver. And considering the fact I had been on the CPR ferry, giving me the benefit of actual sea time, I considered myself a bit of an old hand at this point. I even imagined I had a seagoing swagger.

When we boarded the ship, I noted immediately some resentment from the crew, but as I look back at it now, I can certainly understand why. What ship's company would covet the dubious duty of escorting raw recruits, for five days, every week, around the Bay of Fundy when there were far more exotic ports to be seen?

Everything on board seemed strange, and as I look back now with the (dis)advantage of my advancing years and with my memory getting shorter, I'm wondering where they put us all. I don't remember any frigate I ever sailed on having a mess deck that could sleep an entire division and its sixty bodies. But perhaps it was only thirty of us that went that week.

We sailed around the Bay of Fundy for a couple of days before pulling into the little Nova Scotia town of Antigonish for some shore leave. This was my first opportunity to try out my new sailor suits on the female contingent of the local populace. And even though they had plenty of experience with brand new sailors like me, I was impressed with the reaction I received from these Antigonish girls.

We were treated royally, and I met a young lady that afternoon who invited me to her parents' house for dinner. I was a perfect gentleman; these people were exceptionally friendly, and being in a home with a family atmosphere and a home-cooked meal, after being locked up in basic training, would have made even the worst of men a gentleman.

The seas were rough the next couple of days, like it can be only on the Bay of Fundy. This is where we found out who the

real sailors were. One evening we were standing in the lea of the
funnel, where it was warm, watching the seasick guys getting rid
of their supper. One of the guys, ironically enough a sickbay
attendant by the name of King, was having a bad time. Like me,
he wore glasses, but unlike me, he sported false teeth. And as was
the rule he was wearing his hat. (As new recruits, we had to wear
our sailor hats on deck at all times.) He was just about to feed the
fish, bending over the guardrail, when he grabbed his hat with
one hand and his glasses with the other and let fly. But it seemed
he was short one hand, because he spewed his false teeth over the
side.

At last we were in our final week, looking back over our
shoulders, wondering where the time had gone. The seemingly
insurmountable hurdles that had been placed in front of us when
we'd first arrived had all been cleared, one by one. We marched.
We no longer needed to double-march. After all, ours was the
number one division on the wall, and if we passed all the tests and
completed all our sewing, they would turn us loose on the world
beyond Cornwallis.

Finally the big day, graduation day, arrived, and the anticipation was running high. Schoolgirl giggles erupted here and there
throughout the division, reminiscent of the day of our arrival. It
was almost time for our final Divisions. Our boots were shining
and our uniforms were spotless, and on our heads were the new
round Port and Starboard caps purchased from the canteen
instead of the pill box-looking hats we'd been required to wear
throughout basic training. They had red lining on the inside left
and green on the inside right, indicating port and starboard
respectively. This all stems from the days before rudders when
ships had steering boards, a big paddle that was always located on
the right side of the ship. The ships always tied up to the dock
with this steering board on the outside and the port to which to
disembark on the left side, so naturally they came up with the
terms Port and Starboard. Navies are very strong on tradition, and
these terms have been around since before Queen Victoria's time.

"Okay, men, we're going to be the smartest looking division
ever to pass out of this dump," seemed to be the order of the day.

If nothing else, they had taught us pride and a certain amount of discipline, and we were determined to put it on display that day.

There was a smartness to our step as we marched to the parade square. With everyone in step, arms swung shoulder high, thumbs pointed straight, fingers bent at the first joint, we were each but one part of a single moving body. We marched past the Commanding Officer while the Navy Band played "Hearts of Oak, Men of Steel," and as we marched past the reviewing stand our Divisional Officer shouted out the command "Eyes right!" in salute. You could almost hear our eyeballs click in unison as we snapped our heads right. Then it was over, and with the command, "Dismissed!" we all threw our hats into the air and cheered.

4

Someone once said, "See Naples and die." Well a few of us decided to spend a few of our thirty days leave in Montreal, on our way home to wherever we were from. One of the guys, George Chaif, was from Montreal, and so we figured, "What the hell, we have a connection, so why not."

I won't even try to relate to you what happened, but three day later when my head started to function properly again, I was on the train heading back to Prince George. I was thinking the saying should have mentioned Montreal instead of Naples.

As we rattled our way back across Canada, the thought lingered in my slowly clearing head that a lot of these people I had worked with, ate with, lived with and had become good friends with over the last four months I might never see again. That it is an unfortunate part of life, but it is life, especially in the military.

When I look back on my time in basic training, I can't help but think it wasn't all that bad. I know at the very least it must have changed me, because when I got back home to Prince George I was anticipating a hero's welcome, but oddly enough it never materialized. My mother, however, was extremely proud of her son, and showed him off to her friends at every opportunity.

Skip came home a week later, and we proceeded to get drunk and chase women. We had proven we could get into the navy, and that we were sailors, so we collected our ten dollar winnings and spent it all on beer immediately. Then just about the time I was starting to fall in love again, a sentiment aided in no small part by the beer, Skip dragged me back to reality. "Mel, our leave is almost up. We have to get back to Esquimalt and get ourselves a ship."

We said our farewells and caught the bus with our remaining funds and headed south to the coast and HMCS Naden, the west coast naval base.

When we reached Naden, there wasn't a ship available, so we were assigned to what was called the Manual Party. After Divisions each morning, we would muster at the Boson's stores where we'd be assigned to a Boson's work party. The word "party" took on a whole new meaning in the navy, one I learned intimately and firsthand.

After working there a couple weeks, we became aware of certain jobs that were considered "jammy" jobs. However, being newly appointed sailors, we didn't get a crack at these jobs. These were the jobs the older hands got over us lowly Ordinary Seamen, for whom they were almost out of reach. The navy stuck to this system of seniority come hell or high water, it seemed.

When we were first assigned to the Boson's party, we got just about every dirty job imaginable on the base. Sometimes we would sweep the parade square and sometimes we would wash floors and windows and sometimes, if they didn't have anything else for us to do, we would simply move a pile of dirt from one place to another with the aid of shovels and a wheelbarrow. If we somehow succeeded in moving the pile prior to the completion of our workday, we would move it all back again. As a make-work program it was very effective, and we certainly did move some dirt some days. Now I don't really remember how many times over the next few months we moved that pile, but, if memory serves, I think it contained somewhere in the order of twelve hundred shovels of dirt.

Then one morning after Divisions, having reported to the Boson's stores where we were looking forward to another day on the end of a four-foot shovel, the Boson's Mate called out, "Ordinary Seamen McConaghy and Robbins."

"Yo," we answered together. That was sailor-speak for "Here I am."

"Report to the regulating office and be quick about it," the Mate growled. Skip and I looked at one another. The regulating office was the place they sent you when something was about to happen to you. Good or bad, you never knew until you got there. We marched off at a good clip.

On our way to the regulating office, we happened upon an officer. As was his custom, Skip made sure he was on my left-hand side, and as we approached the officer we snapped off a smart salute, me with my right hand and Skip with his left.

Now everyone knows you always salute with your right hand. This stems from the days when folks carried swords, and to show the person you met you weren't reaching for yours, you doffed your hat with your right. I guess every one was right-handed in those days, but Skip always used his left.

Sometimes the officers would notice something wasn't right and do a double take, but by that time we'd have finished our salute and be marching smartly on our way. They never did pick up on it, and like Skip would say, "What the hell's the difference anyway. They got their damned salute."

That day, at the regulating office, we got ourselves a ship.

Our ship, as she was affectionately called, was the "Big O," the HMCS Ontario. One of two light fleet cruisers in the Canadian Navy at the time, she was the pride of the west coast fleet, all 555.5 feet of her. Her size staggered the imagination of this poor boy from Aleza Lake. Skip just shrugged his shoulders and said, "The damned thing is probably older than my mother." Skip was like that. Not much impressed him except girls, and not many girls at that.

I, on the other hand, was mightily impressed. Along with what seemed like hundreds of smaller guns bristling all over her, she boasted two mountings of three six-inch guns forward and one aft. There were also two mountings of four torpedo tubes on the main deck, amidships. This was a warship then, an 11,130 ton warship, and to top it off there was a crew of 867 officers and men that together formed more than ten times the population of Aleza Lake.

I walked down to the Naden jetty late that afternoon, after dinner, and looked across to the naval dockyard to see her tied up at her berth amongst all the destroyers, frigates, mine sweepers and other miscellaneous watercraft. She had the sun setting behind her, and she stood out like a very large diamond set amongst a multitude of smaller ones.

This was the time in the Canadian Navy when sailors wore black hats and black woollen jerseys under their uniforms in the winter, and when all the ships had dark grey hulls and light grey superstructures, all except the "Big O" and her sister ship on the east coast, the Quebec. In later years, long after this practice was abandoned and we were relating old sea stories to the junior ranks, we would refer to them as "the days of black hats, iron men and two-tone ships." But alas, before we could join our new ship, they sent us on another thirty days leave. I was beginning to think this navy life was quite all right. After all, by the time I'd been in this outfit six months I'd have had a full two months holidays. Add to this the fact that, two weeks after we were scheduled to join the ship, she was to leave on a voyage that would take us down the west coast to San Diego, through the Panama Canal to Jamaica, and up to Halifax before making the long trek across the Atlantic to Portsmouth, England. From there we would travel to Rosyth, Scotland and to Kiel, Germany to take the Kiel Canal to Abenra and Copenhagen in Denmark. Then it was off to Oslo, Norway before heading back to Glasgow, Scotland from where we would steam back down to Nassau in the Bahamas and back through the Panama Canal to Los Angeles before heading home to Esquimalt. And in all these places we would have two, three or maybe four days shore leave if we weren't on duty. Now this might not sound like such a big deal to some worldly soul, but to a boy from Aleza Lake it was one hell of a big deal and I was definitely looking forward to it.

We were still broke from our last leave, and making $93 a month didn't afford us much of an opportunity to accumulate any large sums of cash. And so what do two young men of eighteen do when they are turned out with very little money? They hitch-hike home to their mothers.

This leave, however, went a little differently than the previous one. For starters, people were beginning to wonder if we were really in the navy at all. For sailors, they said, we seemed to spend an awful lot of time in the bush. So we would trot out our uniforms and our somewhat limited seagoing tales, but they were still a little sceptic.

Skip's parents had some money, so he mostly hung around home in Aleza Lake and made the odd trip to town, which usually ended up costing me any money I had saved from working at a service station nearby. Sailors, as a rule, drink and party, so when it came time to head back to the ship, I had to borrow enough money from my sister Shirley for the bus to Vancouver and the Ferry to Victoria. I wasn't yet wise to the fact that all I need do was find my way to any federal government office where they would issue me a travel warrant to return to my ship. I wasn't yet wise to much, it turns out.

5

A warship like the Ontario lying alongside its home port is like a patient lying in a coma in a hospital bed with feed tubes of steam and electricity running into it, keeping it alive in its inert existence.

Then, deep in the bowels of the ship, in one of two boiler rooms, a match is lit. With this match, a torch is lit. Then a stoker lights one of eight burners on the boiler that starts to heat the water, creating steam, the lifeblood of the ship. As the steam pressure increases, more fires are lit, more steam is generated, turbo-generators begin to turn and the ship starts to come alive. Finally, no longer required, the feed tubes are cut. The ship has become a warm, pulsating mass of steel, wire and human flesh as the crew comes aboard, preparing to go to sea.

Skip and I reported to our ship the night before our leave was up. It was late evening, the ship was tied up to the jetty, and the closer we approached the more impressive she became. Her large guns and massive superstructure made her look threatening even though, as we approached, with the gentle humming of her ventilation fan, it sounded as though she were sound asleep. There was only one part of the watch onboard.

We climbed the gangway to the quarterdeck with our duffle bags over our shoulders and our hammocks under our arms. Once onboard, the Quarter Master immediately shouted at us, even though we were only three feet away, which startled me. Skip, for his part, never seemed to get startled about anything.

"What is the matter with you people! Don't you know you are supposed to salute the quarterdeck when you board a ship of war?"

Dropping my duffel bag and hammock, I turned to the quarterdeck with every intention of snapping off a very smart salute, when my foot caught a ringbolt on the deck and I fell flat on my ass. Together the Quarter Master, his Messenger and Skip all broke into laughter, the commotion of which caught the attention of the Officer of the Watch who immediately marched over to us and, with all the authority a brand new sub-lieutenant could muster, asked, "Now just what the hell is going on here?"

As I picked myself up off the deck, saluting anything and everything that was breathing, Skip very calmly explained how we were just joining the ship. We showed them our orders. The Messenger took said orders and handed them to the Quarter Master, who in turn handed them to the Officer of the Watch, at which point the orders were scanned briefly before making their way back to us via roughly the same route.

The Officer of the Watch told the Quarter Master, a salty old Leading Hand about twice his age, to take care of the situation, at which point the Quarter Master told his messenger to take us below to the stokers' mess and turn us over to the Leading Hand of the Engineering Watch. About this time I was thinking to myself, "So this is what designating authority looks like." But then maybe it was just chain of command.

The messenger led us forward from the quarterdeck, out under the massive aft six-inch gun turret and past strange and foreign pieces of equipment, down ladders, along passageways, through corridors, until I was completely, utterly lost.

Finally we climbed down a ladder into a mess deck stretching from one side of the ship to the other, some sixty-three feet. It was equally as long, and held three long tables and four shorter ones with vinyl covered benches on either side. There were half a dozen settees down the port side that paralleled two of the longer tables. The backs of these settees could be swung up at night and fastened to light chains hanging from the deck head, converting them to bunks. Only the Senior Hands got these bunks.

Lockers a foot wide and five feet tall sprung from every available space; this is where we stowed our personal gear. It was immediately apparent that, what had seemed little more than a silly exercise in basic training, that of rolling our gear into eight-inch rolls, was indeed a very efficient necessity onboard a ship.

There were some hammocks strung from pipes that ran along deck head. These pipes were of all sizes, with different types of insulation, and contained electrical wiring that ran fore and aft amid a maze of ducts blowing fresh air into the mess deck from fans that ran nonstop.

The Ontario had been built for the British Navy, and when the British built a warship they had priorities, the first of which was the propulsion: "Let's make this thing go." Then the armament: "Give us all the firepower you can stuff into this thing." And of course along with the propulsion and armament a ship need-ed fuel, ammunition and all the associated equipment to make it work. Any space left over, after they got all this crammed into the hull along with freezers and stores, was for the crew.

With the hierarchy that ran rampant in the navy, the Captain enjoyed what might be considered a suite while the officers had cabins and a wardroom for dining, recreation at sea and entertain-ing while in harbour. They even had their own galley and cooks.

The Chief Petty Officers and Petty Officers had their own messes with bunks along with a mess man to bring their food from the crew's galley to their cafeteria. The mess man cleaned up and more or less took care of them. The space left over was for the hands. They were stuffed in, under and atop any available space that remained.

The messenger turned us over to the Leading Hand of the Engineering Watch, who turned out to be a decent sort of person devoid of the aloofness of those who'd greeted us thus far. This was important, as up to that point of the evening I'd been starting to think that maybe it would be a good time to go AWOL.

The Leading Hand explained to us some of the workings of the mess deck: where the wash places were, where the heads were, and where we could sling our hammocks for the night. The next day, he explained after we'd completed our in-routines, the Senior Hand of the mess deck would assign us to our mess.

The ship had broadside messing, with each of the tables in the mess deck having their own dishes and cutlery. Every mealtime one or two of the junior hands would take large rectangular aluminum pans up to the galley, get the meal and return it to the mess where the Senior Hand would dish it out. If you were fortunate, and were assigned to one of the smaller messes, you received a bigger portion, as by the time the food passed through the hierarchy of the mess, being a junior hand meant you got yours last, whatever was left of it.

That evening we were told to find a spot to sling our hammocks. We would have to live out of our kit bags until morning. It was at that time we learned, or should I say started to learn, about the mysteries of the hammock.

According to history, the hammock has been around for about a thousand years, ever since the Mayan Indians started employing them in the jungles of South America. They were introduced to Europe by Christopher Columbus upon his return in the 1400s, and adopted by the British Navy shortly thereafter. According to most accounts they were hot, sweaty, and far too narrow for comfort. During battle, they would be lashed to the gunwales of the ship to protect the crew from small arms fire. I imagine this would provide some welcome ventilation for its occupant later, should he indeed survive said small arms fire. By the time I got around to slinging my hammock, some one thousand years after its initial conception, with all the modern developments and modern technology that had gone into it, I wasn't any happier than the first sailor who'd slung one. We had played around with them at Cornwallis, learning the basics, but now came the moment of truth: I had to sleep in the damned thing.

I found a spot that looked like it would be out of the way and secured one end of my hammock to a nearby pipe. Then I secured the other end to another pipe and removed the lashings that kept it rolled up in a nice tight bundle. So far so good, or so I thought. It hung there, just above eye level, looking like little more than a canvas sausage, about the same as it had before I'd unlashed it.

I was standing there, trying to figure out how I was going to spread the mattress, sheets and blankets in which I was to sleep, when one of the older hands who'd been watching my performance with a certain amount of pleasure from a bench across the mess came over and said, "You need a mick stick."

"A mick stick? What the hell's a mick stick?" I asked.

"I've got an extra one, I'll let you use it," he said as he walked over to retrieve from his locker what looked like a three-foot length of hockey stick shaft with a V-shaped notch cut in either end. He placed it under the clews (the small ropes attaching the hammock to the steel ring with the line you tied to the mick bars at either end), then took the last two clews on either side and placed them in the V-shaped slot on each end of the stick, holding the hammock open. "A spreader," I thought.

"There you are," he said. "Now you can get in."

"Where can I buy one of these things?" I asked, not wanting to go through the same production the following night.

"You can't. You'll have to make one. But if you want this one, I'll sell it to you for two dollars." I had no idea where I was going to find a hockey stick on a warship, so I paid him half of what remained of my worldly wealth and got myself a mick stick. I think that stick was still with me when I left the navy almost ten years later, the best two-dollar investment I ever made.

Now that my hammock was all set up, all I had to do was get into it, a feat accomplished by grabbing something solid on the overhead and swinging your feet up, followed by your ass, and then finally the remainder of your body.

Now that might sound like a fairly easy manoeuvre, but you have to remember the hammock was designed a thousand years prior to this my first real encounter with the technology.

On my first attempt, I was a little too far away from the hammock, and though I managed to get my feet in I found I couldn't get my ass over far enough to get it in. So there I was, more or less horizontal, suspended six feet above the deck, with my feet in one end of the hammock and hanging precariously from my arms near the other. My only option at this point was to start over. But when I tried to get my feet out of the hammock, it rolled over and spilled my blankets, pillow and mattress onto the deck.

By this time, to no one's surprise except maybe my own, I was starting to collect an audience. No one had busted out in laughter *yet*, but I knew it was only a matter of time. Even Skip was watching, having had the foresight to wait and learn from my mistakes.

By now I was determined to get into the hammock if it was the last thing I ever did. After a couple more futile attempts I finally achieved my goal, and as I lay there amidst a certain amount of satisfaction I realized that after all the exertion and stress I now had to go to the bathroom. Getting out proved to be almost as disastrous as getting in, though I only dumped my bedding on the deck one more time.

That night, even though I was tired from a long day and the frustration of getting into the hammock, I lay there in fear that sometime during the night, in a deep sleep, I would roll over and fall out. Needless to say, my first night aboard my new ship was a rather lousy one. However, over the years, my hammock became a good friend, and when the sea was angry and the ship was bouncing around, twisting and turning, I slept like a newborn baby cuddled in its mother's arms.

That next morning, after a very fitful sleep, I was woken at six thirty by the very loud, very shrill call of the Boson whistle and a somewhat poetic spiel on the intercom calling the hands, a system of communication used in the Royal Navy and the Royal Canadian Navy and just about every other navy in the world to communicate orders throughout the ship.

In the days before electronics, Boson's Mates would be running around delivering messages, but in the modern navy an onboard communication system took their place. There were calls to wake up the hands, to call the hands to dinner, and just about anything else you can imagine them getting the hands to do.

This was a time when the hand making the call could get creative, and if the ship wasn't too pusser ("pusser" in the navy being a term that meant everything "by the book") he could wax poetic. One such wakeup call I liked to use was, "Wakey, wakey, rise and shine! Let go of your cocks and grab your socks, it's morning in the swamps!" This little ditty got me into trouble more than once, but the crew seemed to like it.

That morning was almost a wasted one, as we weren't officially onboard yet, and being as such there wasn't any breakfast
allocated for us. If it hadn't been for some benevolent messmates
willing to share theirs, we might have gone hungry till lunch.

At 0800 hours we went in search of the Cox'ns office and
our assigned In-Routine wherein we would report to all the
ship's departments. It was like a general introduction, letting
everyone know you were onboard and part of the ship's
company.

This wouldn't have been a problem if we'd known the ship,
but as we didn't know the ship, we spent a great deal of time wandering around, back and forth, in search of its various departments. Not helping was the fact that it wasn't uncommon for
some playful hand, when asked for directions, to turn us around
and send us in the exact opposite direction we ought to be going.

At 1100 hours, when the Boson piped, "Up spirits, afternoon
watchmen to lunch," and we finally found our way to our
assigned mess deck, we still had about three departments left to
report to. Later on, when we made our way back to the engineering department and were assigned our workstations and steaming
stations, we officially became part of the ship's company.

In the hull of most warships there was one deck above the
waterline. All the decks below were watertight with no access
between them, but the ones above had watertight doors separating each watertight compartment. Directly aft of our mess deck,
on the starboard side through a watertight door, stood the number one boiler room. It was accessed via an air lock, because if the
pressurized atmosphere of the boiler room wasn't faithfully maintained while the boiler was being steamed, the boilers wouldn't
function properly and a "flash back" could occur, shooting fire out
the front of the boiler. This fact was drummed into your head the
very moment you were assigned to work or steam the boiler
room.

I was very fortunate that my first work and steaming station
was the number one boiler room. The stokers' showers, washroom
and heads were located directly opposite the air lock of the number one boiler, while the galley where we collected our food was

just above the ladder leading up from the mess deck, so the first few weeks I was aboard the ship I didn't really have to worry about finding my way around. Everything I needed or needed to know was in my immediate vicinity, and this gave me some time to get my bearings in my off-duty time.

As our departure date drew closer, a full complement of the ship's company began to come aboard. It soon became apparent there wouldn't be enough room in the mess deck for me to sling my hammock, so I found a spot in the passageway at the top of the ladder leading up out of it. It seemed an ideal spot, right above a hammock storage rack.

It wasn't until a few days later, when I got an itch, that I realized the insulated pipe I grabbed hold of to swing myself into my hammock each night was insulated with fibreglass, and every time I grabbed it little pieces of fibreglass would float down into my hammock. It wasn't long after that I found a little less irritating spot to sleep.

One of the mysteries of the navy, at least to members of the civilian population, was the watch system. Twenty-four hours a day, seven days a week, the ship is manned. I was told that during wartime, in hostile waters, they stood watch on and watch off, effectively dividing the ship's crew in half, but in peacetime it was four watches with one quarter of the ship's company thus engaged at any given time.

Let's start at 0000 hours, or midnight. That's when the middle watch, or mid-watch, comes on. At 0400 the morning watch takes over the ship and remains in charge until 0800, at which point the forenoon watch has the ship until 1200 hours. At this time the afternoon shift or watch takes over until 1600 hours, whereupon things get tricky with the dogwatches.

The first dogwatch goes from 1600 until 1800 hours, and the second dogwatch takes over until 2000, so that the watch keepers can get their supper. Besides, you wouldn't want one group stuck with the dreaded mid-watch everyday. You'd have yourselves a mutiny. So with the dogwatches complete, the first watch now goes from 2000 to 0000, at which point we've rounded the clock and the whole procedure begins again.

The mid-watch was the most hated watch because even if you got to bed at 2000 hours and managed to get to sleep, you'd only get at the most four hours before you had to go on watch. Then, when you got off at 0400, you only had 2$^{1/2}$ hours before the wakeup call was issued, at which point you rolled grudgingly out of your hammock, lashed it up and put it in the mick rack, washed, shaved, ate your breakfast and at 0800 turned to for four hours.

During the forenoon watch, all hands that weren't keeping watch toiled away in their respective workplaces. The morning watch, for instance, having knocked off at 0800 and having thus enjoyed a late breakfast, turned to in the mess deck, cleaning, polishing and scrubbing everything imaginable. Just before up spirits at 1100, the Fist Lieutenant or Commander on the larger ships made the rounds to check and see that everything was shipshape. Furthermore, every Friday morning at 1100, the Captain made rounds of the mess decks, and the one designated the cleanest received a special cake that evening at dinnertime.

The first two weeks aboard went quickly, and before I knew it we were going to sea. I considered myself an old hand by this time, even if no one else did. At least I could get from the foreword end of the ship to the stern without getting lost. Not too many times at least.

Then finally the big day arrived, and early that morning the ship started to come alive. At 0400, the Engineering Watch on duty the previous night started to make steam, getting the machinery up and running. Initially, the boilers used the steam piped aboard via the steam line from shore. Then, when the boilers were operational, the electricity producing steam turbo-generators were fired up, the shore power was cut, the cables were disconnected, and by 0800 the whole ship was a veritable beehive of activity. The engineering staff was busy in the engineering compartments, the upper deck was alive with seamen making ready for sea, and on the bridge the Captain was giving orders.

The telegraph that transmitted orders from the bridge to the engine rooms and the boiler rooms clanged to life. This was it. The orders I'd been waiting for finally arrived: ready main engines, stand by the lines, let go forward, let go aft, slow ahead port engine, slow ahead starboard engine.

As the ship proceeded out of harbour, the ship's company that weren't on watch lined the shipside from bow to stern, and I just happened to be one of them.

There was a breeze blowing, the signal flags were snapping on the yard arms, the sailors' bellbottom trousers and collars were blowing around, and I proudly took my spot along the guardrail with the rest the sailors and snapped proudly to attention as we steamed passed Admiralty Rock, taking the salute from the Admiral in charge of the Pacific Fleet. My dream of going to sea was finally a reality: the boy from Aleza Lake had become a sailor.

That first day at sea, after we had cleared harbour, I went below to change into my dungarees (dungarees were the denim work clothes issued in the navy) and turn to in the mess deck where I would clean and keep out of trouble until they piped, "Up spirits, afternoon watchmen to lunch," at 1100 hours.

This was exciting for me, even a little nerve-racking, as we'd only been at sea four hours and already here I was with an afternoon watch. It wasn't a big problem though, because being an Ordinary Seaman in training I'd have one of the senior Able Seamen on watch with me, at least this time. If I did it right, and they thought I could handle it my next watch, the mid-watch, I would be on my own.

In the boiler room, on the afternoon watch, besides myself there was another stoker as well as a Stoker Petty Officer in charge. The boiler room Stoker P.O. had to attend to the boilers, watching the water level, fuel oil pressure and the boiler room air pressure, but his main job was to make sure the steam maintained its designated pressure. Each boiler had eight fires, or nozzles as they were called, and if we weren't steaming too hard and they weren't using too much steam, you could run with three fires in each of the two boilers. Then, as demand increased, when the speed of the ship increased, the amount of fires in each boiler was increased in order to compensate for the demand.

They didn't make it a guessing game. When the bridge rang down on the telegraph to the engine room for more speed or less speed or any other manoeuvre, it was also indicated in each of the boiler rooms. In this way there were no surprises. Everything that happened in number one boiler room was mirrored in number two boiler room, like a well-choreographed ballet.

Each nozzle or fire was suspended in a round opening in the boiler front on a shaft about three feet long that, when in use, could be pushed into the boiler and locked in place. The hose supplying the hot oil was connected to the shaft on the outside of the boiler front by a quick coupler and a shutoff valve, and when the fire wasn't being used you slid the shaft partially out of the boiler. Each fire was encircled by a damper controlled by two T handles that protruded from the boiler front. When you lit a new nozzle you opened the damper, and when you shut it down you closed it. And if for some reason you forgot to open it, the fire wouldn't burn properly and instead of steam you made smoke.

This was the cardinal sin aboard ship, to make smoke. But if it did happen, you would immediately get a call from the bridge: "You are making smoke. Cease immediately."

Every night during the mid-watch, the officer of the watch would turn the ship broadside to the wind and you'd perform a manoeuvre called "blowing soot." Each boiler contained two parallel pipes with steam jets, and when the steam was turned on and you rotated one of the pipes, it would blow steam onto the horizontal water tubes, blasting any soot from them. Then the Stoker P.O. would turn up the air pressure in the boiler room which, together with the heat from the fires, would carry the soot up the funnels. However, if this little manoeuvre wasn't coordinated with the bridge, you'd end up with black oily soot all over the upper deck and this, to say the least, wouldn't make you a lot of friends in the navy.

6

That first night at sea, when I signed off the mid-watch at 0400, I could feel the gentle roll of the ship beneath me. Well this fascinated me. I mean what kind of sea does it take to make a ship of this size roll? In spite of the fact I was dog tired and should have been going to bed, I made my way up to the upper deck and stood by the guardrail.

By this time we were deep into the Pacific Ocean, well clear of Race Rocks, and as I looked back over the port quarter I could see a faint glimmer of light. Although there were some dark clouds in the sky, I could still perceive the steady undulation of the ocean, and when I looked up over the main mast I could see it moving back and forth in a gentle sway exaggerated by its immense height.

A ship at sea is like a living being. The gentle humming of its ventilation fans pumping air into its body, the soft throbbing of its propulsion and the vibration of its four large screws as they spiralled their way through the water, thrusting it forward, allowed it to take on a life of its own. No wonder we conceive of a ship as a "she," I mused idly.

I knew I should be in my hammock, because 0630 was approaching quickly, but as I stood there marvelling at the utter vastness and the somewhat ironic tranquility of this huge warship steaming along as though she and all aboard her were the only people in the world, I couldn't help myself.

And as I stood there on the quarterdeck watching the wake trailing off behind us and the phosphorescence sparkling like angel dust, this feeling was multiplied by the fact that I was alone under a vast sky with but a scattering of black clouds and only the odd

star glimmering through them, knowing the sun would be breaking over the horizon in but a few short hours. Despite the fact I
was on a ship of war, I was filled with an immense peace. And for
all the years I spent at sea, this would be my special time of day. A
time of quiet. A time to be alone and reflect while most of the
crew were below, sound asleep. This was "my time," no matter
which ocean we were on or what our purpose was for being there.

I must have stood there a good half hour before I realized I
was getting cold and that I'd better get below and get my head
down if I knew what was good for me. When I finally did crawl
into my hammock and lay there feeling the gentle roll of the ship,
I fell into a deep and sound sleep. This was my first experience of
sleeping in a hammock at sea, and it was a sensation I would come
to relish over the next ten years.

The next few days, until we reached San Diego, seemed to
blend together with the nights. You were either at your workstation, on watch or waiting to eat, a routine broken up only by time
spent in your hammock, enjoying the ever-warming weather or
perhaps a movie in the recreational area, sometimes for the third
or fourth time.

Life onboard a ship was, in a word, routine. Everything was
performed according to a routine. At every mealtime, for instance,
a couple of junior hands from each mess deck on the ship gathered in the galley with their big aluminum pans to draw the meal
for their respective messes. Some of the messes were larger than
others, and it took two hands to get it all.

Then everyone sat down while the Senior Hand dished out
the meal, first to the Leading Seamen, next to the Able Seamen in
order of seniority, and finally to the Ordinary Seamen. Then,
when the meal was finished, the selected junior hands filled the
mess deck fanny (a large rectangular aluminum bucket with a
handle like a water pail) with soap and water and cleaned the
dishes, cutlery and mess table.

Another routine, in this case a tradition, initiated in the Royal
Navy prior to Queen Victoria's days, was the issue of $2^{1/2}$ ounces
of Black Navy Rum to all hands, from the Chief Petty Officers
on down. The officers had their own bar in their wardroom, but

much to their chagrin the Navy Rum was not part of its liquor stock, nor was it made available to them.

The tradition was started in order to ward off scurvy, on account of a seagoing vessel's inherent lack of fresh fruit and vegetables. Then, in the days of sail, they would "splice the main brace," or issue every man an extra tot, prior to going into battle to lift his spirits and, I imagine, make the thought of his impending death a little more palatable.

Every morning of every day, when a ship is in commission, at precisely 1100 the Boson's mate would make the pipe, "Up spirits, after noon watchmen to lunch." This pipe not only brought the rum up from the rum locker, but brought up the spirits of the crew about to consume it. Unfortunately the rum was only issued to hands over that age of twenty, and I at the time was only eighteen years old, so I sat in the mess deck with the rest of the underage hands and watched with envy as the older hands drank their rum in front of me. Although Leading Seamen and below were supposed to drink their rum mixed with water at the time it was issued, making a concoction called "grog," most of the tot drinkers would mix it with Coke syrup from the vending machine or save it for some other time.

It is amazing the ingenuity shown by the hands to get away with their rum neat, in order that it might be saved. Rum was nothing if not a bartering tool aboard ship, and it wasn't uncommon to hear one hand say to another, "Can I have your tot today and I'll give you mine tomorrow?" or "I'll give you my tot for a week if you stand my watch for me when we get into harbour."

I remember hearing how one distraught mother had written the captain of a ship, voicing her displeasure at the fact the navy had taught her son to drink. According to legend, he wrote back that it wasn't the navy that taught her son to drink, but she in his infancy when she taught him to drink from her breast. Now I can't really say for certain this actually happened, because according to tradition it was the captain of whatever ship you were on when the story was told who put the mother in her place.

Over my navy career, after I started drawing my daily ration of rum, I really got to liking it and became what was known as a "rum rat." Although the rum was over-proof, I can honestly say I never got into any trouble with it, although later on in my naval career, when I became a Senior Hand and some new hand was joining the ship, coming to me with his in-routine in hand that said "temperance," I would strike a deal. I would give him the ten cents a day the navy gave him for not drawing his rum, if he would be so kind as to draw it for me. After ten years in the navy I figured I owed about 3600 tots of rum, give or take.

I had over a period of time developed a taste for this bitter-sweet, black repast, sometimes but not always called Nelson's Blood. I believe the primary reason I never once in all my years got seasick in a storm was because I had Nelson's Blood in my stomach, or so at least I told myself.

It was always a pleasure to be tied up alongside an American ship in San Diego or Pearl Harbor or wherever, sitting on the quarterdeck in the sunshine drinking rum while the Americans, staring with envy, drank their Coke and ate their Hershey bars. And later in my naval career, while I was on loan to the British Navy and the Rum Boson would draw the rum for the whole mess, I would bend the paper cup at the Coke machine so that I only dispensed the syrup, giving my grog a reasonable taste of rum and Coke. I think I was responsible for breaking one of the many traditions of the Royal Navy. But then rum isn't a drink that should be mixed with water, in my mind.

Anyway, the day we entered San Diego Harbour was a typical bright California day. I was amazed to see oil derricks and hammerhead oil pumps lining the shoreline, and as we entered the harbour I saw hundreds of mothballed warships tied up three or four and sometimes even five abreast.

As I stood along the ship's guardrail for the entry harbour routine, one of the older hands started ribbing me. In fact, from the time we'd left Esquimalt harbour, any chance the older hands got they would rib us younger hands in much the same way. "Wait till you get to Tijuana and one of those little Mexican hookers get their hands on you," this one said in San Diego that day. "That's when you'll become a *real* sailor.

"You know," he went on, "to be a real sailor, you have to have seven tattoos and have had at least five social diseases." Well then I guess I'll never become a real sailor, I thought. And while I did admittedly go on to get a few tattoos, I seemed to miss out on the social diseases. In this regard, some of the training films they had shown us at Cornwallis seemed to have paid off. And I like to think that, at the time, I did have some taste.

At length there came a pipe over the ship's intercom. There would be a "Make and Mend," and the gangway would be open for leave at 1200. A Make and Mend meant that all the ship's company, apart from the day's duty watch, would have the rest of the day off. Of course most onboard had anticipated this, and by the time the gangway opened just about everyone was dressed up in their 2–A uniform (the rig of the day for shore leave) ready to make landfall.

Most of us Ordinary Seamen not on watch were excited about this our first trip ashore in a foreign port, and six of us having decided there was strength in numbers were heading straight for Tijuana.

It has always surprised me how, when a sailor leaves a ship in search of some unknown destination, it doesn't matter how foreign the country, he always manages to find his way there. But that seems to be the easy part. The hard part comes well after he arrives, when, having partied, danced and gotten all too drunk, he must somehow find his way back to his ship in the middle of the night. I think it's a combination of the fact the ship resides in the ocean, the ocean resides at the lowest point of the surrounding landscape, and the sailor, having assumed some of the characteristics of the day's liquid diet, simply follows the path of least resistance back to the ship.

We found our way across the border into Tijuana without any trouble. It was amazing for a kid from a little town forty-five miles east of Prince George to be suddenly getting so much attention from people, the majority of which were trying to sell him things he couldn't even imagine, from plaster bulls to new upholstery for his car and everything in between.

The biggest surprise I got, though, was when this local kid, about nine or ten years old, tried to sell us the services of his virgin mother. Now the only time I'd ever heard anything about a virgin mother was back home around Christmas, so needless to say this little episode left me a little confused at the time.

We wandered around a while, checking out the sights and the many bars and clubs lining the main drag. Unlike at home or in the navy, no one seemed all that interested in our birth certificates. The only thing they were interested in was our money.

This was the first time I had ever witnessed real poverty. I had gown up thinking our family was poor, but some of the deprivation I saw now startled me. What I saw that day made me realize just how fortunate I was to be Canadian. Later in my travels I would see people living in conditions much worse than this, conditions distressing for even the hardened traveller I would become, but that first day in Tijuana shocked me.

After about an hour we ran into one of the hands from our mess deck who told us the place to be was a club just down the street called the Blue Fox. We didn't have any trouble finding it, because like every other bar on the strip the Blue Fox employed a half dozen or so rough looking characters to guide you in.

Once we were inside, and our eyes had become accustomed to the somewhat disconcerting lack of light, we could see there was a stripper on the stage. Now coming as we did from a place called Canada, with our somewhat Victorian morals, this was something of a revelation. And the girls working the floor wore less clothing than most of the girls I had seen in the National Geographic magazine in my high school library.

The stripper onstage was grinding her hips to the very loud music, and I began to wonder if she had any bones in her body at all. The only time I'd ever seen movement like that was watching a garter snake slither through the grass back home.

Meanwhile, the girls working the floor were doing things that made the farm boys gasp in amazement. And every time a new stripper came onstage, everyone would start to holler, "Take it off! Take it off!"

One of the hands from the ship was an Able Seaman who went by the nickname of Bulgy. Now Bulgy came by his nickname honestly. He stood about 5'4" and weighed around 200 pounds, and although he had a bit of a gut, he was pretty well built. But all that aside, and there was a lot of it to put aside, his most outstanding feature was his head of curly black hair.

Now there are plenty of people with a head of curly black hair, but in Bulgy's case this hair grew from the top of his head right down to his toenails. He could shave and two minutes later be sporting a five o'clock shadow. But even his black hair paled in comparison to his voice. Bulgy had a deep booming voice that seemed to resonate throughout any space, no matter how large, he might be occupying at the time. I don't like to say that Bulgy was repulsive but, in a word, he was.

Now Bulgy, like everyone else in the crowd, was hollering, "Take it off! Take it off!" and to no one's surprise, least of all his own, his voice caught the attention of the stripper onstage. She immediately stopped dancing in order to locate where in the crowd the voice was coming from, at which point she called out, "You come up and take it off!"

The one good thing you could say about Bulgy was the fact he wasn't the least bit shy. As mentioned, the rig of the day was what was called the 2–A, so all he was wearing were his bellbottoms and white cotton gun shirt. Well no sooner had the siren's call gone out and Bulgy was jumping up onto the stage to gyrate right alongside her. Then he grabbed the neck of his gun shirt and, with one sudden jerk, ripped it off. The sight of his large hairy chest and stomach brought a few gasps from the crowd, but when he reached down to undo his fly and drop his bellbottoms to the floor, the place went dead, as though everyone had suddenly turned to stone.

There stood Bulgy in all his glory, with a big grin on his face and his pants around his ankles. Bulgy was in the habit of not wearing underwear in the warmer climates—"Too damn hot," he used to say—and there we were faced with the end result.

It took a few minutes for everyone to recoup their composure and, in turn, for the festive atmosphere to regenerate, but when Bulgy sat down it was to a rousing round of applause. Thankfully someone found him a shirt to wear before any lasting damage was done to either the stripper's profession or to ourselves. I was told later that, when he returned to the ship, the Officer of the Watch simply shook his head at the sight of Bulgy in his colourful Mexican shirt with a look on his face that said, "I don't even want to know."

I have to report that my little sojourn across the border brought me no closer to assuming the status of a "real sailor," what with no tattoos and no social diseases to report. And so, lacking the funds to continue my Tijuana way of life, the next two days were spent touring some of San Diego's more civilized points of interest, and after four days it was back to sea, heading south to the Panama Canal. Still, the trip down the coast was that much more interesting with the stories of the crew's adventures in Tijuana.

7

The further south we steamed, the hotter it got. Eventually the temperature inside the ship was making sleep uncomfortable, so I had to find a spot a little cooler in which to sling my hammock. One of the best spots on the ship, surprisingly or not, was in the torpedo bay with its big sliding doors that opened up on each side of the ship, effecting a comfortable cross-breeze. Unfortunately, being a little slow on the uptake and greener than grass, by the time I realized I should be looking for a better place to sleep most of the spots in the torpedo bay had been taken up by the older hands. They'd been down around this latitude before, it seemed. Some had camp cots made of steel rods and canvas that worked well, except for the fact they now had to find a place with shelter. The overhang under the back of the 6–inch gun turrets was an ideal spot for a camp cot, but here again being a junior hand meant I hadn't yet picked up such valuable information.

The morning we entered Panama Harbour, around 0800, it was a hot sunny day with a light breeze blowing in from the sea. A light swell made the ship roll ever so gently as we entered the harbour manning the side in white shorts, gun shirts and sandals. There we stood along the ship's guardrail, and having come from the north in early spring, all our tender pink Canadian skin stood exposed to the cruel furnace of the tropical sun.

We tied up in Panama City for a couple of days, and the gangway was opened at 1200 hours for shore leave. According to the navy, getting a sunburn was considered a self-inflicted wound, but in my mind making us stand out there in the blazing sun all morning was akin to some kind of torture. When I put my socks and boots on to go ashore, I was in a tremendous amount of pain, and I was not alone in my misery.

We walked around the city a while, checking out this and that, before eventually finding our way to the USO canteen. None of the older hands would ever be caught dead in a place like this—not enough action for them—but I didn't have much money, so I didn't think blowing what little I had on booze and whatever other sinful endeavours such minimal finances would permit me was an appropriate course of action.

Started by a number of religious organizations during the Second World War, American Armed Forces Service Clubs were run by volunteers for the entertainment of servicemen. This particular club had a canteen where you could get free non-alcoholic beverages and sandwiches, and there was a big dance floor with an old jukebox in the corner. There were girls too, nice girls from nice local families, and I met a real Latin beauty by the name of Candy Lea Vions. Candy's father was a local judge and her family was very well to do, and we had ourselves a terrific afternoon. We danced, and when we weren't dancing we were talking. We talked about Panama and the heat and we talked about Canada and the snow. She was fascinated with the idea of snow, and if she hadn't seen it in pictures probably wouldn't have believed it existed.

That evening, when the club was shutting down, Candy asked me to meet her down the street. When I questioned why we couldn't leave together, she told me the rules of the club forbid the female volunteers from leaving with the guests, so I agreed to meet her a block away. We walked and talked, and she showed me some of the sites including a beautiful tropical park where we sat on a bench beside a waterfall and did the things young people will do on a bench on a warm tropical night. Then we had to leave, she for home and me for the ship, so we kissed a long lingering kiss and parted after agreeing to meet the following afternoon.

I lay in my hammock that night, afraid to go with sleep for fear I might not wake up the next morning and miss our rendezvous, a somewhat ridiculous notion considering the racket onboard the ship come 0630 hours.

The next morning, the four hours I had to work in the forenoon seemed to drag, but the agonizing wait was eventually rewarded with a fantastic afternoon at the beach. From the shoulder bag she was packing, which seemed to contain just about everything imaginable, Candy produced a bathing suit for me and one for herself that was much less a bathing suit and more like a very skimpy bra and underwear.

In this part of the world the bikini was commonplace, but for a kid from Aleza Lake it was a revelation and didn't leave a hell of a lot to the imagination. What a contrast of colours we were, she with her deep bronze tan and me with my patchwork of red and white blotches. No one would be mistaking me for a native anytime soon.

Just before dinnertime, Candy took me home to introduce me to her mother, father and younger sister. The mother and sister were very pleasant towards me, but I seemed to detect a certain amount of coolness from the father, which was understandable considering the circumstances. And later, when the women left the two of us alone, the atmosphere changed from cool to downright cold when he inquired into my religion. I told him, and couldn't figure out quite what the problem was until Candy returned me to the ship in her mother's car later that evening, at which point she informed me her father was a devout Roman Catholic who wasn't about to let his daughter get mixed up with, in his words, "some damned Protestant Canadian sailor."

The Ontario was set to sail the next morning, so we said a very long goodbye and vowed to stay in touch by mail, which we did for quite a long time. I, of course, was devastated by this turn of events, having loved and lost again, but by the time we reached Jamaica I had recuperated enough to feel ready for whatever new conquest lay in my path.

The trip into that locks of the Panama Canal, and through the Canal itself, was quite an experience. Any ship going through must be capable, at any time, of generating full power. This meant both boiler rooms had to be ready to provide full power for the engines, which in turn meant we had to maintain steam in both boilers. The forced draft fans were at an idle, barely turning over, and in the tropical heat the temperatures in the boiler rooms hovered around 120° Fahrenheit.

Under these circumstances, the boiler room and engine room watch were changed every fifteen minutes, though some of the hands, overcome with heat, couldn't make it that long. Oddly enough though, I realized the heat didn't really bother me. Sweating is the body's built-in air-conditioning, and I happened to sweat profusely.

Be that as it may, I didn't spend all my time in the boiler room that day. I would stay down for a half hour or sometimes an hour, and then I would go up on deck. The ship's band was playing on the upper deck as we entered the Canal, and the men that worked the locks were dancing around, having a good time.

This was the first time I heard the song, "Cherry Pink and Apple Blossom White." The trumpet solo, and the ability of the band to play it that afternoon, has always stuck in my mind, and even today when I hear that song it brings back the memory of the Panama Canal and the girl I'd met and left behind. But considering the fact this was back in 1955, I now hear the song less and less every year, though the memories it produces are compounded by time.

Following the Canal, we sailed northeast for Jamaica, and after three days at sea entered Kingston Harbour. Although Kingston, like Tijuana, was a tourist destination, there was a remarkable difference between the two. Kingston had the same tourist stores and street vendors, but unlike in Tijuana they were clean and civilized. We went ashore in a group again, hitting a couple of bars where we were well received, as we were in just about any port in any country in the world, eventually ending up at the Pyramid Hotel. It was a pretty ritzy place, what with its enormous swimming pool boasting a swim-up bar normally reserved for guests, but because we were Canadian sailors we were welcome to use it. Needless to say, the three days we spent in Kingston were quite enjoyable. Making a paltry $96 a month, you never really had the money required to travel in style, so you made do with what you had and with what the locals gave you, many of whom would take you under their wing and show you around.

The day we left Jamaica was one of those bright beautiful Caribbean days, and later that evening the sky was a delicate light blue with not a cloud in sight. I shall never forget that night, sitting on the upper deck. There was a soft breeze blowing across the ship and a long rolling swell beneath her. The main mast was scribing arches back and forth across the endless sky, and the sapphire blue of the sea surpassed anything I had seen in my life. The sun sat like a bright red ball on the horizon, refusing to go down, while the surrounding sky mimicked its fiery intensity. Every hand that wasn't on watch was out there lounging around, but there was hardly a sound. Only the soft, throbbing breathing of the ship herself touched the ear.

No wonder men fall in love with the sea. She can be like a temperamental lover, one moment warm and gentle and tender, holding you to her bosom, and then, with what seems little provocation, turn angry and cold and menacing, tossing you from her bed in a rage. And as we made our way north, out of the Caribbean and into the Atlantic, sure enough the skies darkened, the sea became angry, and the wind brought with it a chill that only a jilted husband or boyfriend would be familiar with.

By this time, when it came to slinging their hammocks for the night, most of the hands were back in their regular spots below decks. I, too, had made my way below again, as the spot I'd found on the upper deck I soon realized was exposed to any squall that happened to come along during the night. More than one night of late I'd woken up with my feet wet and the bottom half of my hammock drenched.

Back to the sea routine. Back to the days and nights of morning watches, mid-watches, turning to in your workspace and cleaning up the mess deck. Looking back, one day seemed to run into the other in an endless parade of navy life in which time held little meaning. But it was not unpleasant, because you settled into a routine and you always had your time off, either on the mess deck or on the upper deck with your shipmates, each of whom had a tale to tell about their last adventure ashore in the previous port of call.

In the evenings there was usually a movie showing, but even these became part of the routine. They'd been brought aboard in Esquimalt, and by the time we reached Halifax we'd seen them enough times we could talk right along with the actors, word for word.

We pulled into Halifax on a dreary day in a drizzling rain. The clouds were hanging down around the surrounding hills, effectively cloaking the city in silence. This was Halifax. Over the years I don't think I've ever seen Halifax on a nice day. I mean I'm sure they have them, but I've certainly never seen them.

Our time in Halifax was spent primarily storing ship and performing planned maintenance, a routine broken up here and there by the odd run ashore. But unlike in those exotic ports down south, in Halifax, a navy town, we were just another bunch of rowdy sailors run amok.

Eventually, though, we took leave of Halifax, and the trip across the Atlantic took seven days. Although we encountered some heavy seas, the voyage came and went without incident, and it was back to the same old sea routine once more. Fortunately we had exchanged our movies in Halifax, so we had a fairly good choice again.

The day we entered the harbour in Portsmouth, England I just happened to be on watch in the boiler room, so I never got ashore, and the next morning I had to suffer all the stories from the hands that had. Fortunately, that afternoon we had a Make and Mend and the gangway was opened at 1200, so it was off the ship and away we go. The most impressive thing in the Portsmouth Naval Dockyard was the HMS Victory, Lord Nelson's flagship. She was cemented into an old dry-dock, preserved for prosperity as a historical site, and she had to be the biggest damned sailboat I'd ever seen. This should come as no surprise however, considering the fact that in Aleza Lake I can't actually remember seeing a sailboat of any size.

Much to my buddy Skip's dismay, I insisted on going aboard and having a look around. It was hard to believe the size of her. It was a wonder that something built of nothing but wood could possibly hold together in rough seas, and the massive amounts of sail she carried on her towering masts must have put an unbelievable strain on her rigging and hull.

Below decks you had to bend your head down to move around. I can just imagine the crew down there, pulling the cannons back and forth with block and tackle, packing heavy bags of powder and loading huge cannon balls at a mind-boggling pace, all of it while bent over at the waist. I could see now why they called those the days of "iron men and wooden ships."

I could almost picture it in my mind, the toiling away on one of these gun decks in the heat of battle. The smell of gunpowder in the air, the roaring of cannons, the powder monkeys running back and forth, and the hollering and the screaming as the enemy splintered timbers and ruined men with return fire. The chaos and blood and noise would be overwhelming, and all the time these men would be bent at the waist, tending to their guns, firing them, oblivious to what was happening around them. A perfect example of what discipline and training could accomplish in the worst of conditions, I decided.

I also decided I would like to spend a little more time on the ship and have a further look around, but Skip was anxious to get ashore to have a look around for something a little livelier and less masculine. Skip went his way in search of women while I spent a good two hours poking around, marvelling at this gigantic war machine from the past.

The galley stove was one huge black monstrosity set on a six-inch bed of rock with a stove pipe rising up through the deck. It was beyond me just how the ship's cooks could conjure enough food for over a thousand men on something like this.

On deck everything was huge. The masts were about four feet in diameter at the base, and the rope lines, of which there were seemingly miles on board, I couldn't get both hands around.

Finally, though, my wandering and dreaming came to an end, and I decided to see if I could catch up with Skip. Before he had left, he had pointed out a little pub just outside the Dockyard gate where we could meet, so I rambled on over. Well there was Skip, already captivating three old ladies with his charm, and I thought

I'd better get over and rescue him, or them, but when I got closer I realized he was just entertaining the old gals, occasionally
quizzing them as to where the best place would be to find some
sweet young things for his own fun.

After about an hour in the pub, we ventured off in search of
the first place, or should I say, the closest place on the list the ladies
had provided us. By this time we were starting to feel pretty good,
and trying to reserve some of our capital we'd taken to drinking
a concoction known locally as "Scrumpys." Turns out Scrumpys
was cheap apple cider that only cost six pence a pint, and at that
price a little bit of money could go a long way. Unfortunately it
could also go a long way to securing you the granddaddy of all
hangovers the next day. I was told you could peel paint with it, or
remove rust, and that it was an excellent remedy for hemorrhoids.
Still, despite all warnings, in 1959, while on loan to the British
Navy, I spent a month in dry-dock in Portsmouth, and by that
time I had a wife and family, so when the funds were getting low
and it was getting close to payday, I would head over to this little
pub and partake of its deadly brew.

Late that afternoon, in one of the pubs the three ladies had
directed us to, I met a young lady. She was very pleasant, had herself a great sense of humour, and was quite good looking. The
really nice thing about her was the fact she didn't drink, so we
danced, talked and laughed, none of which cost me any money.
The time went flying by, and next thing I knew it was 1115, which
meant I'd have to run like hell to get back to the ship before midnight. Before we parted company, though, we made arrangements
to meet the next afternoon at the common, or local park, around
1400.

Now at this point one might be wondering why a young single sailor in the prime of his life had to be back onboard his ship
by midnight. I mean is he some kind of Cinderella or what?
Actually, the fact I was an Ordinary Seaman, and underage, meant
I was, in fact, a Cinderella, and therefore required to be onboard
by 0000, or in laymen's terms, by midnight. It's pretty hard for a
guy to be either a lover or a drunk when he has to be back
onboard his ship by midnight. This particular rule or regulation

or whatever you want to call it was really cramping my would-be swashbuckler's style.

I arrived at the common around 1230 the next afternoon, so I had some time to kill. I had a cup of coffee and walked around a while, but the aftermath of the previous night's Scrumpys was really taking its toll. So I lay down on the grass and had a little nap.

One nice thing about the sailor suit is, at a time like this when you want to have a nap, you just lie down on your back, flip up your big collar so you won't get any grass stains on it, then lay your hat down as a pillow on top of it. No matter how you mistreated it, the old tight-fitting round rig always looked good coming out of it.

I fell asleep soundly, and when I finally woke up, there she was, my date, sitting beside me putting daisies in my hair. I spent a very pleasant three days with this one, though being Cinderella I unfortunately cannot say nights. Once again I was in love though, despite my continued lack of nocturnal accomplishments.

After leaving Portsmouth, we steamed a couple of days up the east coast to the Firth of Forth in Scotland to tie up at a little British naval base called Port Edgar under the south end of the Fourth Bridge, one of the Seven Wonders of the World. There was a little town called Rosyth nearby, where it just so happened the father of the girl I would eventually marry was born. Of course I didn't know this at the time, and it wouldn't have made much of a difference if I had, because there was nothing in Rosyth except a few quaint fieldstone cottages with straw thatched roofs, with not even a single pub to shake things up a bit.

Although this was a pretty spot to be tied up in, what with the natural beauty surrounding you and one of the most famous architectural structures in the world hovering there above you, it just wasn't the place for a rambunctious young Canadian sailor like myself.

There was a wet canteen on base, but I was still underage, so if I didn't want to stay onboard or hang around the base, which I didn't, I had but one option: catch a little ferry across the Forth and then catch the train to Edinburgh.

The train took just under an hour, at which point we did the tourist thing a while, seeing Edinburgh Castle and eating fish and chips, and afterwards downing a couple of drinks and wandering around. But being on a tight schedule, we hustled back to the train station and caught the train back to the Forth Bridge, then took the ferry over to Port Edgar. The last ferry was 11 o'clock— the next one not running until seven o'clock the following morning—so being on Cinderella leave we really had to play the game.

I was on duty the next night, so I never got ashore that day, but the third day we had a Make and Mend so off we got to an early start. It just so happened to be payday as well, and with a few bucks in our pockets we decided to do a little partying in Edinburgh. The usual debauchery ensued, though I'm afraid we partied a little too long, and by the time we caught the train and reached the ferry dock it was almost 11:30, which meant we'd spend a long, cold, dismal night trying to sleep on an open jetty.

One of the guys came up with a bright idea. If we walked across the bridge, he said, we'd still be late, but at least we wouldn't have to sleep outside. We considered it, but then figured the ship would probably have left by the time we got to the other end. That and the fact we had no way of knowing if there was any place to walk up there.

When we got back to the ship the next morning, to no one's surprise we had been marked "adrift," so we went on Commander's Report. When we got up in front of the Commander and told him our story, all he said was, "It is your responsibility to be back onboard the ship at the designated time," and then gave us seven days of Number Five Punishment. This meant we'd have to work two extra hours each of the next seven nights and that our shore leave was cancelled, which was no big deal as I was broke anyway.

The next day we dropped our lines and set sail for the Kiel Canal in Germany. The Ontario was the first Canadian warship through the Canal, and although we never stopped in Kiel, it wouldn't have done me a damned bit of good if we had, as I was still on punishment.

8

Our next stop was Abenra, Demark. It wasn't a very big place, and didn't have birthing facilities for a ship this size, so we just anchored in the harbour. When we arrived I still had two days of punishment, so my Abenra entertainment consisted of looking over the side and wondering what the guys were doing ashore.

The last day in Abenra was a visitors' day, which meant some of the townsfolk could come out to the ship for a tour. Being on punishment still, I of course was assigned tour guide duty, which consisted of leading some folks around the ship and explaining as best I could exactly what we did. I was given a young Danish family to show around, a man in his 30s, his wife and his daughter, and the wife's prettier, younger sister.

These were nice people, and the sister was nice to look at, so I showed them a few things that weren't on the designated tour. I took them into the mess deck and other such places, spending extra time with them, because they were such good people and the sister and I were getting along so well.

When we got back up top, they asked me to come ashore. They wanted to show me some real Danish hospitality, they said. I explained how I'd been a bit of a bad boy in Scotland and how, for a few days more, I wasn't allowed to go ashore. The husband told me, if he had a chat with whoever was in charge, he'd be able to get me permission to come visit them at their family home. I tried to explain that I didn't think there was any possibility of them letting me go. About this time the wife's sister was getting extremely friendly, and as much as I wanted to go ashore with them and be alone with her, I thought maybe it wouldn't be such a good idea to have her brother-in-law marching up to the Office of the Watch and demanding my release.

As they were leaving, the sister took me in her arms and gave me a long kiss and later, as I watched their boat leaving, I almost cried. I have thought about this many times over the years, and fantasized about what might have happened if I had been allowed to go ashore. Anything might have happened. And I would have fallen in love yet again of course.

Our next port of call was Copenhagen, and by the time we arrived my punishment was up, so I was free to explore one of the friendliest and prettiest cities I'd seen to this point. The usual four of us went ashore and spent a good part of the day just looking around and marvelling at just how many beautiful blonde women there were. Later that afternoon, after downing a few ·drinks in different bars, we ended up at one where we were served by a young waiter from New Zealand who was working his way around the world. We were feeling pretty good when the waiter said to us, "You know, even if you guys came in here without uniforms, I could still tell you were Canadian."

"How would you be able to tell?" one of us asked.

"Well it's like this," he said. "If someone comes in and looks around like he wished he owned the place, I know he's English. If he comes in and looks around as though he did own the place, I know he's a Yank. But when you Canadians come in, you don't really give a damn who owns the place."

Looking back at this statement now, I'm thinking it could have been an insult, but at the time and under those conditions we thought it was a compliment so we gave the guy a cheer and carried on with our party. Being the poor young Canadian sailors we were though, we didn't have the money for tips, so the cheers were all he got from us that day.

The next day we decided to visit the Tivoli Gardens, one of the biggest permanent circuses in the world, and what a circus it was. Most of the day and a good part of the night were spent picking up girls. You would meet what seemed like a friendly pretty girl, and then another one would walk by who seemed that much friendlier and prettier, so you would desert the one and go chase after the other. We spent the entire day running around in circles this way, and when it came time to return to the ship there we all were, looking at one another, dumbfounded and exhausted from our pursuits but no better off than we'd been when we first came ashore.

The next day we were a little wiser in our approach, and formulated a plan of sorts. We would pick one girl out and pursue her, and if we succeeded we'd put imaginary blinders on. This, we thought, would be the only way to succeed in our pursuits, instead of chasing around in circles like a bunch of kids in the proverbial candy store.

I spent the following day walking around Copenhagen with a very lovely young lady I'd been pursuing the night before, and later that evening we went to her home where I met her mother and father. Sometime during the conversation she asked me if I'd like to go swimming, assuming she meant some nice heated pool. I told her I didn't have a suit, as it wasn't something I'd normally pack, and she told me as she left the room, "That's not a problem, you won't need one."

I was sitting in the living room of her parents' house when she said this, and I could feel my face start to go red right there in front of her parents. I was speechless. There was silence. And when she finally returned, it was with a beach blanket and towel, and as she walked by she reached over, grabbed my hand and led me out the door, cheerfully saying goodbye to her parents over her shoulder. I, too, was looking over my shoulder with what I assume was a very stupid grin on my face. I tried to muster up a little goodbye, but the best I could come up with was a shy little wave.

By the time we got to the beach it was dark. I remember the lights of the city twinkling across the little waves while she undressed and ran into the water with a scream of delight. After a few minutes of self-loathing I finally stripped down and followed. I jumped in and immediately jumped out again. Swimming in the Baltic on a chilly night in April might be an exhilarating experience for some, but for me it was anything but, and I probably set some kind of land-speed record for the time it took me to hit that water, realize how cold it was, and return to the beach and cower under the blanket.

I was a perfect gentleman that night, though admittedly not by choice. As quick as it was, my little plunge into the frigid Baltic waters had reduced my manhood to near nonexistence, and by the time I got the blood circulating in all parts of my body Cinderella syndrome was rapidly setting in. If I was late returning to the ship again within a month of the previous charge, I wouldn't see shore again until we were back in the Pacific Ocean.

I can still see her, standing there in the moonlight with the water running off her body while I scrambled, franticly, to get into my uniform, mumbling something to the effect of, "I'm sorry. God am I sorry. But I have to go." Common sense had prevailed over passion yet again, and I regretted it for years. The next day I was too embarrassed to even meet her, so I stood in for one of the other guys, taking his watch. Even in a big city like Copenhagen I was afraid I would meet her again, and what would I possibly say. I was told later by one of the hands that he'd seen her in Tivoli Gardens looking for me. I felt like a jerk, and still do to this day. The least I could have done was take the time to explain how I had to be back onboard the ship by midnight, instead of leaving her standing naked on the beach wondering what was wrong with her.

The next day we set sail for Oslo. Like most of the Scandinavian countries, Norway was a great place to visit, and its people treated us like kings. The guys were ready to make an impression on the local girls, but as I was still distraught from my disastrous escapade in Copenhagen, I went ashore with one of the married guys instead. We did a little sightseeing, he did some shopping, and we met some nice people who invited us back to their home for dinner.

Being in such a home, eating such a nice relaxing dinner with such warm and friendly people, brought back memories of my own home and family in Aleza Lake, and when I returned to the ship that night I sat up on the upper deck a good long time. For the first time in what seemed like a long time I was truly homesick.

Visiting one of the city's many museums the next day, I met a young woman with whom I spent a pleasant afternoon. That evening, when we parted company, she gave me a little kiss on the cheek, and as I walked back to the ship I was feeling a little more at peace with myself.

The next day we sailed for Scotland, and so it was back to our at-sea routine. I hadn't seen too much of Skip in Copenhagen or Oslo, and one day while we were sitting on the upper deck looking out to sea he said to me, "What the hell did you get up to back there. I've hardly seen you at all."

I related to Skip my Copenhagen adventure in all its glory, and he almost fell over he was laughing so hard. "She probably thought you were gay," he blurted out, holding his sides in laughter. I had always known Skip wasn't the most sensitive person, but from that point on I learned to keep such embarrassing escapades to myself.

Leaving Norway, we sailed around the top of Scotland into the North Atlantic and down to Greenock where we eventually tied up. Being only about twenty miles from Glasgow, that's where most of the hands spent their time off.

I was still feeling pretty awful, but I went ashore to have a look around anyway. After roaming around a couple of hours, looking at nothing in particular and starting to get hungry, I wandered into a little pub for a pint and something to eat.

From its appearance, this pub had been around a long time. There were two rows of wooden booths on the left, and the bar ran parallel to the booths towards a little dance floor in the back. It was about 1500 when I walked in, and I was the only person there besides the old gentleman behind the bar. I sat down across from him and ordered a pint of ale and a menu. As he placed my pint down before me he said, "You're one of the Canadians off the ship that just tied up yesterday, down at the quay?"

"Yes, sir," I said.

"During the war we had a lot of Canadian soldiers stationed here. This place used to be packed with you boys every night. If you go and have a look at the booths you'll still see their names and addresses carved in most of them."

After ordering a sandwich, I took my pint and had a look around. There had to be hundreds of names carved into those wooden booths, from every Canadian province, city and town I had ever heard of. Some had little messages scratched in along with the names.

I don't really know how long I spent looking over all the names and talking to the old barkeep, maybe a couple of hours. He reminisced about the things he'd seen and the laughter he'd heard in this place, but inevitably the question was posed: "I wonder just how many of those boys who carved their names into these booths never made it home?"

I can remember there being a long silence until finally the old barkeep said, "A lot more than either you or I want to think about, I'll bet."

It wasn't long afterwards that people started shuffling in, and the old barkeep introduced me to some of the older patrons. They were eager to reminisce about the war and the Canadians they'd met at the pub, pointing out one name or another carved into a booth and saying something like, "I remember him, he was a fine young lad," followed by the inevitable question, "I wonder if he survived?"

We left Europe three days later, steaming straight back across the Atlantic to Panama City. We only stopped in Panama a few hours though, so I never got a chance to get in touch with Candy, the girl I'd met there two months previously. I did get a birthday card from her on my nineteenth birthday, though none of my letters were answered. Eventually I got a letter from a friend of hers saying how her father had placed her in a very strict Catholic boarding school after I'd left.

After Panama, we sailed up the west coast to San Francisco. I was bored by then with my quiet gentlemanly lifestyle, and headed for the beach with Skip and a couple of my old running mates as soon as we were allowed ashore. It was time to let off a little steam, and although we were still underage, we weren't having too much trouble getting into bars.

Later that night, we ended up in a bar with a chorus line of some of the most beautiful women I had ever seen. Or so I thought, until I found out they were running the same kind of equipment I was.

I was a big boy now, something of a world traveller who knew such people existed, but this was something completely different. Certainly I'd never seen so many at one time under such peculiar circumstances, and it would be some time before I'd be able to look at a beautiful woman again without a certain amount of hesitation. As it was, I left San Francisco a little wiser and a little more sceptical for the five-day journey back to Esquimalt.

This is when I first ran into a phenomenon known as Channel Fever. It started out slowly with a lot of the married hands and those with girlfriends sitting around the upper decks at night staring out to sea with faraway looks in their eyes. Then, as we got closer to home, they began to take out the gifts they'd bought for their families, placed them on the mess deck tables, and inspected them thoroughly. The married men scheduled to be on duty the day we arrived were bartering with single men to stand their watches. "You stand my watch when we get in and I'll give you my tot for a week."

"A week? Hell, Smitty offered me his for two weeks."

"Ok, two and a half weeks then."

"It's a deal."

Nothing was sacred, and the more ambitious single hands even went so far as to demand money.

The day we entered Esquimalt Harbour, I stood in for one of the hands, a guy who'd been good to me and with whom I'd traded some watches on the trip. He was an Able Seaman, but I'd gotten my watch-keeping ticket on the cruise so I was able to stand in for him.

I wasn't on watch that morning, having stood watch from 0400 to 0800, so I was required to put my uniform on and man the shipside as we entered harbour. It was a beautiful late spring morning, the sun was shining and there was a light breeze blowing as we pulled in alongside the jetty. The Naden band was playing some cheerful tunes, and the jetty was lined with wives and girlfriends in summer frocks blowing lightly in the breeze, some with children clutching the hems of their dresses, all trying to find their loved ones manning the shipside.

You could feel the excitement when someone spotted their significant other. The wife would wave, the children would jump up and down calling, "Daddy, Daddy," and fathers seeing a new son or daughter for the first time would weep openly. But for me, as I had no one, although it was exciting to see the married hands milling about in anticipation of the gangway opening, it was a sad time. In fact, until I got married and had a family of my own, this would always be a sad time for me, and eventually I went down to the mess to join the rest of the single hands wallowing there in loneliness and self-pity.

9

On December 2, 1955 I was drafted back to HMCS Naden to take my Trade Group 1 Course, my first step towards becoming an Able Seaman. The course itself wasn't too difficult—we studied steam engineering, diesel engineering and some basic math, all of which proved fairly straightforward as we'd already learned much of it onboard—and on the 10th of February, 1956 I passed, getting promoted to Able Seaman shortly thereafter. No longer at the bottom of the pecking order, I had become an old salt with "sea time," which meant of course that it was time for me to start belittling the new recruits coming in from Cornwallis.

It was around this time I was starting to come to grips with the fact that discipline itself was not my enemy. Without discipline a warship couldn't function properly: if every man onboard a ship did not obey the orders relayed down to him through the chain of command without question, then everyone onboard that ship and the ship itself would be in jeopardy. This revelation, though long in coming, would serve me well throughout my life, especially when dealing with anyone in a position of authority.

I worked a short period of time on the Boson's party, but this time around I was a little better positioned and got some of the better jobs around the base. This only lasted until March 1, when my orders came in and I was drafted to the HMCS Cedarwood.

The Cedarwood was a warship. Not that she looked like a warship or acted like a warship, but she was in fact a warship, at least according to public record. A ship made out of wood—a novelty in a navy of steel—she was 120 feet long, pointed at both ends, and looked like a fish packer. She always reminded me of the boat in Farley Mowat's *The Boat Who Wouldn't Float.*

She was a little different than the Ontario, what with her crew of sixteen officers and men, but she was a blast to serve on, a veritable comedy on water.

The Cedarwood was launched in 1941 in Lunenburg, Nova Scotia, the same place as that other famous Canadian boat, the Bluenose. She was christened the J.E. Kinney before being drafted into the Royal Canadian Army Service Corps and renamed General Schmidlin, her primary duty the supplying of army detachments at scattered harbours around the Maritimes and Newfoundland. Then on September 22, 1948 she was commissioned to the RCN for oceanographic survey duties on the west coast and renamed HMCS Cedarwood. The captain was a Lieutenant Commander with considerable seniority. The problem was he didn't seem to have all his oars in the water, and thus consistently found himself being passed over for the bigger, more glamorous commands.

The Cedarwood came equipped with several quirks that made it quite unique when it came to handling, but the worst was probably the engine. Installed in 1944, it was what was called a direct reverse six-cylinder diesel engine, which meant the engine was connected directly to the propeller shaft. When you wanted to stop the ship by reversing the engine, you first had to change the engine's cam setting by pulling a lever, but not before the engine had come to a full stop. Well, when the ship was still moving, the momentum of the ship turned the propeller, which in turn turned the propeller shaft, which turned the engine, which was a very bad thing.

They partially rectified the problem by installing a 1500-pound flywheel with an air-operated brake on the back of the engine. So now the new routine was to stop the engine with the brake on the flywheel, change the cam setting to reverse mode and start the engine again, this time rotating in the opposite direction. This worked pretty well, but it took time, and the captain, thinking he was piloting a destroyer, would come into the jetty a little bit hot, putting on a show for anybody who happened to be watching. At the last second he'd call for reverse main engine, and with that old Cedarwood it just didn't happen that quickly. Consequently we had a habit of running into things, especially the dry dock gate.

Any time we were coming into our normal birth in front of the dry dock caused a certain amount of anxiety, more so if there was a ship in it. Those in the know would try to have the dry dock flooded when we arrived, in the faint hope we wouldn't damage anything, but even this wasn't foolproof when it came to the old Cedarwood.

Old Jim was a Chief Petty Officer, Second Class Motor Mechanic. A throwback from the old Royal Canadian Naval Reserve, he should have retired after the Second World War when that organization was officially disbanded, but somehow he slipped through the cracks in the bureaucracy and landed himself a permanent position here on the Cedarwood. Old Jim had been onboard forever, and whenever we entered and left harbour he was always the man in charge of the engine room.

When orders would come down from the bridge, say a "Finished with Main Engines," crazy old Jim would look at the engine room telegraph and say something like, "The captain doesn't want that. No, he wants a 'Slow Astern.'" Needless to say, the combination of a showboat Captain and a crazy old Chief often made for some pretty exciting manoeuvres, and I was always glad I wasn't on the upper deck while these manoeuvres were taking place. They were embarrassing for everyone concerned.

When I sailed on the Cedarwood, she was used primarily as an oceanographic survey ship. This meant we sailed up and down the west coast's inside passage loaded with oceanographers and their scientific equipment, shuffling in and out of inlets and sounds, testing sea currents, temperatures and whatever else the eggheads wished to waste time and resources on. Still, as far as duties went, this was a pretty good one, as it gave us lots of time to lie around the upper deck taking in the sun.

One time we were coming out of Seattle. It was a nice calm day as I remember, and the waters in the Strait were like a mirror. I went up top to get a breath of fresh air at one point, and saw an American fishing boat steaming abreast of us on our port side. When I returned to the engine room, I told the old Chief about it. He stood there a few minutes beside his trusty old engine with a look of concern on his face, and then finally said, "Go up, have a look, and see if we're making any headway on her."

I went up the ladder, stuck my head out of the hatch and had a look, then went back down. "No, I think she's making a little headway on us, Chief."

He stood there about fifteen minutes, still looking concerned. Then finally he turned to me and said, "Go and have another look."

I went up, had another look, and sure enough she was overtaking us. So I went back down and reported, "She's gaining on us, Chief. Not by very much, but she's definitely gaining."

"This is bullshit! We're a Canadian warship, we can't have some damned Yankee fish boat overtaking us," he said, and reached for the throttle. Now while the old Cedarwood was capable of doing 9 knots at 550 RPM, at this speed there was a lot of big iron flying around inside the engine. Ask any more of her and she might just fly apart. As well, after estimating our speed and course, the Navigating Officer had sent our ETA ahead to the flag office in Esquimalt based on 320 RPM once we'd cleared harbour, which we were doing now. Still, not about to be outdone by a fishing boat, the old Chief reached for the throttle and cranked on a couple more revs. "If we do it a little at a time, they won't notice the change," he reasoned. "Go up and have another look."

My next two hours were spent running up the ladder, having a look, coming back down and telling the Chief that she was still overtaking us or that I thought we were holding our own. Shaking his head and swearing, the Chief would crank on a couple more revs regardless.

Now, with all this extra speed, when the Navigator would take a sighting and calculate our position, he'd find we were well ahead of our ETA and ring down to reduce the revolutions. The Chief, in turn, would answer the telegraph, shake his head, and send me up top to see how we were doing.

At one point the Navigator sent one of the crew down to see what was going on. When the seaman entered the ear-splitting noise of the engine room, the old Chief put his arm around his shoulder, smiled broadly and shouted into his ear, "Its okay, son, we're homeward bound!"

The seaman smiled and left. Everyone onboard wanted to get home early to meet their families, except for the Navigator, who only wanted to meet his ETA. Only on a ship like the Cedarwood would you find a silly situation like this.

Eventually, when the fisherman changed course, much to the old Chief's pleasure we were outrunning her, though admittedly not by much. Maybe the skipper on her didn't know he was in a death race with a Canadian Man-of-War.

Another time, we were deep-anchored off Diamond Island just outside Hecit Strait with a string of sixteen very expensive hydrophones strung out on our anchor cable. Meanwhile, the James Bay, one of our inshore minesweepers, was running out to sea on a triangle course dropping grenades so the oceanographers could check how sound travelled underwater in that particular area. Everyday we received the weather radio transmission at 1400 hours, but on this particular day our radio communicator had found his way into the rum and was sound asleep by the time they transmitted the weather: a storm was brewing and we should head for shelter.

The old Cedarwood was condemned for open water, so when the James Bay came steaming over the horizon signalling for us to hoist our anchor and sixteen very expensive hydrophones, there was a bit of panic onboard.

The sea had already started to snarl, and the seamen had to scramble to get all the rigging in, and by the time we were under-way the storm had already settled in. The poor old Cedarwood was bouncing around violently as we ran flat-out at our maximum 9 knots.

An hour later the sea was really heavy, and each time we came over a big swell and down the other side we buried our bow. The old Cedarwood was at this time in her life a pretty tired old ship, and with all the bending and twisting she was taking in this heavy sea, she started to take on water.

Below deck, water was running in through the cracks opening up in the deck. Our bedding, our clothes, everything was getting soaked, and across the mess deck water ran freely. The cook, who was chronically seasick and onboard because we so very seldom got into heavy sea, was locked away in his tiny galley. Braced against the cupboards, he was the colour of freshly picked peas, and about as sick as I have ever seen man or beast.

Even though everything in the galley had been properly secured, no one had expected this kind of sea, so there was the cook, in his lifejacket, pressed into a corner with flour and whatever else cascading down upon him, his silly grin turning to agony whenever his stomach pitched over. The large pot of soup he'd had going on the galley stove had spilled over and mixed with the water running across the deck.

The bilge pumps were powered by electricity, and the two diesel generators were on the portside of the engine room with the switchboard directly between them on the bulkhead. The water, however, was rising faster than the pumps could handle it, and soon it reached the bottom of the big flywheel on the back of the engine. The flywheel, in turn, started throwing water up onto the switchboard, shorting out the power and consequently shutting down the bilge pumps and the rest of the ship's power.

This was a problem no one had ever anticipated. Still, there was a big hand-operated bilge pump on the starboard side, just in front of the engine room hatch on the main deck, and every man that could be spared was up there taking turns at it. Not much prompting was required to get people to work the pump when you explained that if they didn't work the pump, and work it hard, we might possibly sink and they would die.

By this time a little panic was starting to set in on the bridge, and the Skipper sent out an SOS. The only ship close enough to do us any good was a US Coast Guard ship that had been steaming south about five miles away from us in the Pacific. The James Bay was of no help to us. An inshore minesweeper and not really built for this kind of sea, she was having her own difficulties.

"My good God," shouted the old Chief over the noise of the engine room, "now we have to be *rescued* by the Yanks."

When the Coast Guard ship finally got to us, she took up position on our windward side, taking the brunt of the storm. Once we were in her lee, everyone breathed a sigh of relief. We steamed along like this for two hours; it was still rough, but with the ship settling down we were able to get rid of some of the water, and before long the generators and bilge pumps were back online.

We steamed into a little bay where the Coast Guard ship dropped anchor and we tied up alongside. They gave us some hot food and some dry clothes, and after we'd showered and dressed they helped us get the old Cedarwood back in shape. All our wet bedding, along with everything else in the mess deck, was taken to their ship's laundry where it was washed and dried. We worked throughout the night getting the ship ready to steam home, down the Inside Passage of course.

Not long after returning home, one of the hands onboard, Leading Seaman Bob McLaughlin, lined me up with a blind date with his sister-in-law, Barbara. He had described her to me and I thought, "Well, nothing ventured, nothing gained," though he told me she wasn't too keen on guys with glasses. So when the big day arrived, as was arranged, I went to meet Bob and his wife Doreen at their place. Along with their new baby girl, Debbie, we caught the bus down to Doreen's parents' place. They were going to babysit Debbie, and Barbara was living at home with them at the time. As we approached the house, I made sure to tuck my glasses into my jumper pocket. I also made sure to carry Debbie. Might just as well make a good first impression, I thought.

As we entered the house, Barbara's mother, who in time I'd come to know as one of the sweetest women I would ever meet, greeted us at the door. Her dad, Jim, was sitting in an easy chair watching TV. When we were introduced I remember thinking, "This guy doesn't seem too impressed with me. But then again," I thought, "I'm not going out with him, I'm going out with his daughter. So to hell with him."

Barbara was in another part of the house, doing whatever it is girls do when they are about to meet a blind date for the first time. When she eventually came into the room I was immediately impressed with her, although in truth, when she looked me over, she didn't seem all that impressed with me. Little did I know at the time that this was the woman who would bear my children and be my wife for fifty years and counting.

After dropping Debbie off, we caught the bus and went uptown to a movie, *The Birds and the Bees* with George Gobles. I didn't see all that much of the film, but not for lack of trying. It was a very large theatre, and we were sitting about three quarters of the way back, and so while they were watching the movie, with my glasses in my pocket I really wasn't watching anything. This truly was a blind date for me.

Soon afterwards, the Cedarwood made its way to Bellingham, Washington where I visited Mary, my mother's older sister. They had a farm just outside of town, and they were having a barbeque in my honour.

Aunt Mary's boys were loggers and pretty husky men, and they liked to drink. They had a big washtub full of beer and ice, from which they kept passing me bottle after bottle. "It's not as strong as your Canadian beer, so you'd better have another one," was their reasoning. We drank all afternoon, and by the time they got me back to the ship, she was just starting to pull away from the jetty.

My cousins unloaded me from the pickup, and with one smooth motion threw me onto the ship where I was caught by several shipmates. True to form, the Captain never looked back, and was unaware of what was happening, while the other three officers on the bridge reputed to have seen my somewhat improvised boarding manoeuvre chose to ignore it. Their willingness to turn a blind eye was explained to me later by the Navigations Officer: "Too much paperwork, and who would believe it anyway?"

We made our way north through Active Pass. It was a sunny day, and there was a lot of traffic on the water, mostly pleasure boats and fishermen. As it was so narrow, navigating Active Pass was always a tricky proposition, made more so by a tide that ran a full 9 knots, matching our top speed. If the tide was running against us we'd be at a standstill, and if it was running with us we'd charge through with wild abandonment. That day the tide was running with us.

Now the Cedarwood in her declining years was like a little old lady, anything but wild. And when we came charging around the corner to meet the ferry from Victoria coming the other way, with our stern swinging this way and that, the crazy old Captain seemed to panic and started giving orders to the helmsman at such a rate that the helmsman just stood there with a look of stark disbelief on his face. "Just what in hell do you want me to do, sir?" was all he said.

The Captain didn't answer. No one moved. Meanwhile, the ferry was closing in. Finally the Navigator stepped forward. "Just steer us out of this, Helmsman," he said. "You know what to do. May I see you in your quarters, sir," he added, and together he and the Captain disappeared into his cabin behind the wheelhouse.

I was the Engineer's Writer at the time, and just happened to be on the bridge getting information for the log. I quickly left the bridge to relay what I'd witnessed to the rest of the crew who were completely unaware of it, although some had been wondering about our recent erratic course.

On October 17, 1965 we decommissioned the old Cedarwood. A couple of days prior to the ceremonies, we returned to harbour after a trip to Seattle flying our decommissioning pennant. Every ship in the Royal Canadian Navy would fly such a pennant on her final voyage into harbour.

I don't really recall what the formula was for the length of the pennant, though I think it was ten feet for every year of active commission. I do know that our decommissioning pennant was at least one and a half times longer than the ship, and there was a lot of discussion about how we were going to trail our pennant behind the ship without dragging it in the water.

Eventually one enterprising young seaman came up with a brilliant idea, and before we left Seattle a couple of the hands went ashore to the US naval stores to explain our situation and retrieve a tank of helium.

The day we entered harbour, we filled some condoms with helium and tied them to our decommissioning pennant. As we steamed into harbour, our decommissioning pennant streamed proudly behind us suspended by good navy issue condoms, proving once and for all and without a doubt the serviceability of such items.

10

The HMCS New Glasgow was one of the Prestonian Class frigates originally launched during the Second World War as River Class frigates, built to replace the old corvettes. They were larger, longer, faster and had a far better range than the corvettes, and they were far more seaworthy and comfortable.

After the war, a total of twenty-one were modified to Prestonian class. This included adding a bigger bridge, a taller funnel and new guns, and inclosing the quarterdeck to house two Squid antisubmarine mortars. More importantly, a cafeteria was added, along with bunks to replace the hammocks. The Prestonian was a very comfortable class of ship, in other words.

They were 302 feet long by 37 feet wide with a draft of 12 feet, and came with a crew of 140 officers and men. They were a good seagoing ship on the whole, though in a heavy sea, with those long Pacific swells, they had a tendency to roll over one wave and dive straight into the next. This wasn't too bad, except for the fact that second wave would almost bring the ship to a shuddering halt while everything aboard her, including the crew, was compelled to continue forward.

Although I didn't spend too much time aboard the New Glasgow, it was time enough to realize that frigates were the ships I wanted to serve on. The one thing that appealed to me the most was the engine room. The twin engines were very large, triple expansion steam engines capable of 5500 horse-power between them. Designed some time before the First World War, these engines were certainly antiquated, but they were almost a work of art in their operation. For one, all their working parts were visible.

Each engine contained four cylinders, with the high-pressure cylinder, into which the steam from the boilers fed, being the smallest. The intermediate cylinder was larger in diameter and had a longer stroke because, after the steam left the high-pressure cylinder, it started to cool and expand and thus lose its power. By the time it got to the low-pressure cylinders, one on either end of the engine, the steam was normally working on a vacuum created by the condenser that cooled the steam and converted it back to feed water for the boilers and very large vacuum pumps on each of the condensers.

To get an idea of their immensity, each engine was about 40 feet long and stood two decks high. When you were on watch, standing on the deck plates between the engines, your feet were level with the center of the crankshaft while the tops of the cylinder heads were about 16 feet above. Steam was injected into the tops and bottoms of the cylinders with the piston rod coming out the bottom of the cylinder through a steam-tight gland. Here the piston rod connected to the crosshead that attached to the connecting rod that attached to the crankshaft. Cams on the crankshaft connected to smaller versions of the connecting rods operated the slide valves, timing the engine, making sure everything worked together and ran smoothly.

Everything, as I said, was in plain view, so when at sea and the engines were running it was like a symphony of steel with everything moving in different directions while working together in seamless precision.

When at sea, there was a Petty Officer, a Leading Hand and either an Able Seaman or a senior Ordinary Seaman on watch in the engine room at all times. One of the Leading Hand's jobs was to run the evaporator, an enormous distilling unit that converted seawater to freshwater for both the ship's company and the ship itself.

This feed water for the ship's boilers was critical. It had to be 100% pure or salt would build up in the boiler tube, just like scale in a teakettle. As for the domestic water, it could be percolated out of one of those old kettles at astronomical speed. To test the salinity, you simply tasted it, and we would have little competitions amongst the Leading Hands to see who could make the most water in a watch.

The only gauges to watch were the steam pressure and the vacuum. To check the temperatures of the crossheads, the main bearings or any other working part, it was simply a matter of leaning over, sticking your hand in and feeling it. The port engine rotated clockwise while the starboard engine rotated counter clockwise, and standing between these two massive engines you could watch the reciprocating motion of the pistons rods change to the rotary motion of the crankshaft right before your very eyes. Other ships, like the destroyers, employed steam turbines where everything was enclosed, and although it was a lot neater and cleaner, it certainly wasn't as spectacular.

One of our missions aboard the New Glasgow was the Queen Charlotte Patrol, which was exactly what it sounds like, sailing up and down the west coat of the Queen Charlotte Islands searching for indications of Russian activity in the isolated inlets and harbours that lined this long and otherwise undefended coast. It was said that Russian submarines had planted hundreds of underwater listening devices all along our coast, and it was our job to catch them. Now while we didn't find the places where they had planted listening devices, we did find the places where they had come ashore to pitch barbecues and smoke cigarettes, because they never cleaned up their mess. Thus, we had to do it. It was as though they were laughing at us, which I'm sure they were.

On one such patrol we spotted a Russian trawler just outside our territorial boundary, and we were ordered to shadow it. This so-called trawler had so many antenna and radar devices sticking out of her that it was a wonder she didn't sink from the pure weight of it.

During the day, they would steam along slowly just within visual range, and then they would turn and come steaming back alongside us. They would stand on deck and wave and smile at us like old friends, but as soon as night fell they would shut off their running lights and disappear. The next morning they would show up again and steam along with us, playing games with us, having a good laugh. Their so-called trawler was at least 10 knots faster than the 22 we could manage.

Shortly thereafter, I took thirty days leave and went home to see the family. It was around the first part of November, and one night in the local legion one of the members asked me if I would represent the RCN at the Remembrance Day ceremonies. "Sure, why not," I said. At this point of the evening I was feeling a little drunk and, as a result, awfully patriotic, and as the request came with a double round of drinks I was up for it.

Remembrance Day 1956 had to be one of the coldest, windiest days on record. That morning, as I looked out the window of my sister Shirley's home, I thought, "This is going to be one of those days I will want to soon forget."

I put on my uniform and fought my way through the wind and down to the legion where they gave me a little fortification to help ward off the cold, and then it was off to the cenotaph. My uniform consisted of a pair of shoes, a woollen winter jersey, my sailor hat, a pair of light leather gloves and a heavy winter overcoat. I stood at ease while every minor politician, veteran and other would-be dignitary who didn't have any idea what was going on did his thing.

The wind was whipping around my exposed ears and up my bellbottom pants, and I was starting to fear that my private parts would be frostbitten before this was all said and done. My mind was running rampant, trying to think about anything except how cold my body was. Finally the order was given, "Dismissed."

"Oh my God," I thought in a state of panic, "I don't think I can move. Will I become a permanent part of the cenotaph? Will people walk by years from now and say, 'There's Mel McConaghy. He *volunteered.*'"

Finally I got moving, at which point the powers that be took me back to the legion where they filled me up with antifreeze for the remainder of the day.

Later that evening, an ex-Sea Cadet took offence to the way I was wearing the lanyard on my uniform, so I invited him outside to settle the matter. On my way out however, I was waylaid by a couple minutes of conversation, and by the time I finally got outside a friend of mine named George had taken care of the guy. I never did forgive George for that. George had lost an arm in a hunting accident earlier in his life, and I'm sure that if George could take this guy with only one arm, I could have beat him with two, finally winning a fight.

The next morning I found out I had been drafted.

In 1956 the Egyptian government nationalized the Suez Canal after Britain and the United States refused to help finance the Aswan Dam Project. In response, the British, French and Israelis invaded Egypt, which led to a bloody conflict and destabilization of the region. In time the international community would condemn their actions, and Egypt's claims were eventually upheld.

After the invasion, the United Nations dispatched peacekeeping forces to the Canal Zone. The contingent from Canada was to be from the Canadian Army Service Corps, but rather than ship the troops and their supplies via freighter, the Canadian government decided to transport them on the HMCS Magnificent—or the "Maggie" as she was affectionately called. On loan from the British Navy at that time, and stationed in Halifax, Maggie was a light fleet carrier of the Majestic Class 630 feet long and 80 feet wide, weighing some 19,550 tons fully loaded. When in fighting trim, she would carry a crew of 1200 officers and men.

The Canadian government, in their infinite wisdom, had decided that twenty west coast ratings would be part of Maggie's crew for this next evolution, ten cooks and ten stokers. I was one of the ten stokers, though of course I couldn't tell anyone. For some reason there was a great deal of secrecy involved.

They herded the twenty of us into HMCS Naden, placed us in our own secure area in the barracks, and left us there to wait. This whole evolution was a bit of a joke; we didn't do an out-routine when we left our ships and didn't do an in-routine when we got to Naden. They even cancelled our shore leave until a couple of days before they shipped us out. Of course everyone around the barracks knew exactly what we were doing and where we were going, but the ruse continued anyway.

The first thing I did when I did get ashore was buy an engagement ring. Then I went directly to Barbara's home and asked her to marry me. It wasn't a very expensive ring; at the time I was only making around $100 a month. I then told her I was headed for Egypt for what was, at this point, an undetermined length of time.

Barbara accepted my proposal. I thought at the time she didn't seem all that excited at the prospect, but considering the fact I'd just hauled her out of bed, asked her to marry me, and then told her I was taking off halfway around the world for God only knew how long, I can understand her lack of enthusiasm.

The next day, December 19th, six days before Christmas, I received my first introduction to the RCAF and an aircraft called the North Star. A DC–6 with Rolls Royce engines, it had to be about the noisiest thing I had ever encountered. It was also the least comfortable aircraft I have ever had the experience of flying in. As a matter of fact, in all my travels, it had to be the second noisiest mode of transportation I have ever encountered. The first being a submarine, or more specifically, in the engine room of a submarine, while travelling on the surface.

They loaded the twenty of us onto the North Star at Patricia Bay Airport, just North of Victoria, and we began our trek across Canada. This particular aircraft didn't come equipped with seats. All it had were two pieces of pipe running fore and aft along the bulkheads with pieces of canvas slung between them, not unlike small deck chairs. As you can imagine, these were just about the most uncomfortable seats imaginable to be flying across Canada in. An exercise in modern torture, the North Star was.

Most of our gear, duffle bags and hammocks were piled in the middle of the floor between the two rows of "seats." The majority of us ended up lying on the floor, on our gear, trying to get comfortable and maybe even some sleep. I have found over the years that if you are uncomfortable and bored, the best way to pass the time is to go to sleep or get drunk.

A few of us had the foresight to bring a few bottles of rum aboard. One guy from Winnipeg phoned his brother and asked him to pick up whatever he could to replenish our spirits when we landed there to refuel. So, for some of us at least, the trip turned out to have a bit of a festive, if uncomfortable, atmosphere.

The powers that be did have the foresight to stock us with bales of cheese sandwiches, even if, after a mouthful of one of these creations—no doubt the handiwork of some Air Force cook who probably had better things to do than prepare our meals— you kind of wish they hadn't. Consisting of two pieces of stale white bread with great quantities of butter and one lousy, thin slice of Kraft cheese, they left a great deal to be desired.

We made our second and last fuel stop in Montreal before carrying on to HMCS Shearwater, the naval air station outside of Halifax. Although it was a big deal back home, somebody had apparently forgotten to tell the people here that we were coming, because when we arrived, just around midnight, they shut down the engines, the aircrew went home, and there we sat in freezing weather with no heat, waiting for someone, anyone, to come get us.

After what seemed like hours, a bus came, picked us up and dropped us off at the ship, but with nobody expecting us and most of the crew on Christmas leave, we ended up sleeping on the cafeteria tables and benches. And, as luck would have it, our luggage never caught up to us until the following day.

The next morning the ship fell into a state of confusion. The cooks weren't expecting us, so there hadn't been enough stores brought up to the galley to feed another 20 hands. Luckily, there happened to be a couple of resourceful cooks on duty, and with the cooks we'd brought with us from the west coast helping out in the galley, we finally got fed.

We sat around the cafeteria until just after lunch when the Chief Cox'n came in, angry as hell for being called in from his Christmas leave, to get us settled into our appointed messes. The fact we'd been there all morning and that nobody knew about us meant they hadn't brought up any rum for us at lunchtime either. Well this was more than we could handle. Here they had yanked us out of our home base over the Christmas holidays and put us on an antiquated aircraft for the most uncomfortable ride imaginable, then abandoned us at what seemed like a deserted air base in order that we might freeze our butts off, at which point they made us sleep, fully dressed, in our uniforms, on the cafeteria tables, and now they had the audacity to forget our *rum*? Mutinies had been staged over a less insulting set of circumstances than this one.

After we bitched and complained enough to the officer on watch, he finally agreed to go down to the rum locker and get us our tots, the only bright spot in the last two days.

The stokers were assigned to the mess known as the "Snake Pit." It was disgustingly dirty, so after lunch we got into our recently arrived dungarees and went to work on it. East coast ships had the reputation of not being as clean as west coast ships, and Maggie was no exception. When we started scraping out the corners, we found they'd simply painted over dirt and dust. If this happened on the west coast, someone's head would roll.

We worked all that afternoon and a good part of the evening after supper, and when no one showed up the next morning to assign us to any particular duty, we carried on cleaning up the mess deck.

This was my introduction to the cockroach. Now certainly I had seen cockroaches before, but then not in such quantity and not of this size. And at night, after lights out, with only the night lights allowing you to make your way around, you could open up your locker and see your gear moving around. When taking out a clean pair of shorts or socks, you made sure to shake them out thoroughly. Unfortunately I can attest to the fact that cockroaches will bite you when given the opportunity.

Once, while working in the Chiefs and Petty Officers cafeteria, I found a cockroach that had to be two inches long. We tied a string around it and tried to teach it to lead, but it was too stupid. One of the guys had read, at one time or another, that if you cut off a cockroach's head, it would live for a week before starving to death. At the time it seemed like a good experiment, and being bored as hell we tried it. He was right; it did take a week.

The following afternoon, the regulating Chief Stoker assigned us to watches and workstations, but seeing as the regular crew was still on Christmas leave, we didn't do a hell of a lot. We worked on the mess deck until noon, and then went ashore and drank beer all afternoon at a pub just outside the dockyard gate. Here they charged 11 cents a beer while back home it was only 10 cents. When we inquired as to the difference, we were informed the extra penny was for breakage, so we started breaking the empty glasses against the table legs. The bartender objected, and eventually we reached a compromise: we would stop breaking glasses and he wouldn't call the police.

By the time the ship's company returned to the ship, the old Snake Pit was sparkling like a new quarter. It was a showpiece—the regular crew couldn't believe it—and from that point on until we left the ship we won the cake every Friday after Captain's rounds.

Once the crew got straightened away, I was assigned to one of the two boiler rooms until just before we went to sea. Then I was assigned to the bread room, along with another west coast stoker by the name of "Tread" Atkinson. Tread had come by his nickname quite by accident. By that I mean he'd earned it. While in basic training, while sewing his name on all his rigging, he managed such a lousy job that when someone tried to read his name, all they could come up with was "thread, thread, thread" which eventually morphed into "tread." As a result he became Tread Atkinson, his actual given name having become all but obsolete by this time.

The bread room was a small compartment just off the cafeteria. Here we stored the bread fresh from the bakery, and sliced it with the mechanical bread-slicing machine. Our job was to slice all the bread required by the ship's company. The bread-slicing machine was considered a piece of ship's equipment, and therefore had to be run by engineering staff. We were also in charge of issuing all jam and peanut butter to the lower deck hands, which made us very important people indeed. Both Tread and I were more than willing to issue an extra tin of jam or peanut butter for the price of a tot of rum, and consequently became known as the Bread Room Mafia, efficiently corrupt in controlling the distribution of these very valuable commodities. When the galley closed after dinner, normally the only thing left out was bread, which of course we controlled. The toasters were accessible to all, but no one likes to eat dry toast.

Once we got things figured out, we found that in four hours one of us could slice enough bread for the entire crew. That meant one day Tread worked four hours slicing bread, and the next day it was my turn to do the same. I think this was probably the easiest job I ever had in the navy, and old Tread and I sliced our way from Halifax, through the Strait of Gibraltar, past Malta to Port Said, Egypt and all the way back to Naples, Italy. I'm sure we were the only two people in the world who could make that claim.

Although the Maggie had cafeteria-style messing, we still had to sling a hammock, which wasn't a big deal for me; I quite enjoyed it. As for all the army personnel, they and all their equipment were assigned to the Aircraft Hangar Deck, which had been separated into three compartments by two fire curtains. Metal bunks were installed in the first hangar, welded together three high, but unfortunately they'd been put in crossways, which meant that when the ship rolled, it was like sleeping on a teeter-totter. We soon discovered there was no better way to make a soldier seasick than to make him sleep on a teeter-totter.

The second hanger was used for their equipment, trucks and whatever else they were going to need in Egypt. The third hangar contained two Dehavolline Beaver aircraft with their wings removed. When we got to Egypt, all they had to do was put the wings on and fly right off the flight deck.

Just after New Year's we got underway, destination Port Said, Egypt. This was to be no luxury cruise; we were men on a mission headed straight for our destination. We sailed across the Atlantic at 20 knots, through the Strait of Gibraltar and directly to Egypt in nine days, refuelling mid-voyage via a British tanker in the Mediterranean. The trip across the ocean wasn't rough by North Atlantic standards, but it was rough enough to make an awful lot of soldiers seasick. Ironically, on the days it was a little rough out, there was a lot of room in the cafeteria, while on the smoother days it became crowded, as most of the hands actually enjoyed the rough weather.

The day we arrived in Port Said was a typical hot dry Egyptian day, and as we pulled up to the buoy we were tying up to it was apparent, from the various ships that had been sunk in the harbour, that there was definitely a conflict of some sort underway. After our lines were secured to the buoy on the fore-word end of the ship, a tugboat pulled our stern around and secured it to another buoy aft, where we would sit for the next two weeks. The next day they brought a barge out alongside and started unloading the army equipment.

Every morning a crew of Egyptian stevedores brought the barge out, and they were always accompanied by a guard of Swedish soldiers. The Swedes carried stockless machine guns slung over one shoulder and across the chest on polished leather straps, and they always seemed to have them at the ready. I was fairly confident the Swedes didn't understand Egyptian and that the Egyptians didn't understand Swedish. Still, when an Egyptian seemed to be headed in the wrong direction, or didn't seem to be doing what he was supposed to be doing, it didn't take much for the Swedes to shout him down while pointing a machine gun in his face. A machine gun, I concluded, made a very good interpreter.

During the two weeks we sat in Port Said, the powers that be arranged for guided tours to Cairo and to the pyramids. It was forbidden for anyone to stray from the tour, understandable considering the fact that in our uniforms, except for the blue berets and armbands of the United Nations Peace Keeping Force, we looked a hell of a lot like the enemy.

Egypt, as a whole, had never appealed to me, so I stayed onboard. I didn't think I'd enjoy tramping around in the sand looking at things I'd already seen in National Geographic, and taking a ride on a stinky camel was definitely not my idea of a good time.

One night, after they'd cleared out one of the hangars, they set up the stage and had a couple of Egyptian belly dancers perform. By this time we'd been onboard for just over three weeks, and hadn't seen a woman in too long.

It was an interesting show. The girls were a little overweight, and boys being boys we did a lot of hooting and whistling, more to make the girls feel good than anything, and maybe to let off a little steam.

They also allowed vendors to set up little markets onboard, accompanied as always by the seemingly ever-present Swedish guards. I brought my one and only souvenir of Egypt at one of these markets, a nicely finished camel's saddle that had been formed into a footstool. I proudly packed the damned thing halfway around the world, all the time imagining the look of delight on Barbara's face when I got it home. But alas, it never happened. By the time we got back to Halifax whatever it was they'd stuffed the seat with was stinking so bad I threw it overboard. It was probably just as well. When I told Barbara about it, thinking she might be a little disappointed, she very flatly asked me, "What would I want a stupid camel saddle for?"

We did have one exciting day in Port Said, the day they put the wings on the two aircraft on the flight deck. The first pilot to fly off was a lieutenant, and I don't think he realized what a short distance these aircraft could take off in. He started his takeoff from as far back on the flight deck as possible, and by the time he got to the island (the superstructure that houses the bridge and the command post on the starboard side of the ship) he was airborne, and a slight crosswind caught him. His right wing went up and his left wing went down, just catching the ringbolts used to tie parked aircraft down. Anyone who wasn't on watch at the time was watching from the anti-aircraft gun sponsons just below the flight deck. From that vantage point, it looked like he was going to crash into the island, but he disappeared behind it, dropped off the side of the deck, pulled her up and flew unsteadily away.

A sergeant was to fly the second one off, and I think he must have been a little smarter than the lieutenant, or perhaps he'd simply learned from the lieutenant's mistakes, because he started halfway down the flight deck, dropped off the end, and flew away as smoothly as can be. Needless to say, the main topic that afternoon amongst the lower deckhands was how a lowly non-commissioned officer took off without a hitch while the Flight Officer himself nearly crashed.

At night, when boredom set in, we'd go up on the flight deck and enjoy the fresh, dry evening air. Up in the hills, behind Port Said, we could see the muzzle flashes from the artillery and hear the distant booming of exploding rounds, a stark if distant reminder of why we were there.

After the army left the ship and settled onshore, it was time to leave. Someone had decided that after our mad dash over there to spend two weeks sitting in harbour, it would be nice for the crew to spend a week of rest and rehabilitation in Naples, Italy.

The rumour running around the ship at this time was that our skipper was trying to get the ship posted there permanently. For what reason I can't imagine; maybe as a floating hotel. The Maggie had been stripped of her guns and the aircraft, and with no Swedes onboard anyone could have taken her over with a switchblade.

When sailors are in Naples there is no such thing as rest and rehabilitation. We probably would have been better off taking our chances with the Egyptians. For instance, one day four of us spotted a carriage being pulled by a small, broken-down horse. One of the guys, being from Calgary and considering himself something of a cowboy, decided we should take this outfit for a ride, chuck wagon style. Through a lengthy conversation and some awkward negotiations with the little old Italian driver, we purchased the carriage for 2500 lira. We even got a bill of sale. However, I think something must have been lost in translation, because by the time the Naples police, the US shore patrol, the British shore patrol and our very own Canadian shore patrol caught up to us it was explained that the old fellow thought he was signing an autograph. He should've known sailors never ask for autographs.

I don't know if it was the traffic violations or the misconception that we were horse thieves or simply a misunderstanding, but they all seemed pretty upset when they caught up to us after a wild ride through the streets of Naples. After a lengthy chase, culminating in a skidding halt about four inches from the end of the jetty with everyone converging on us, the Italians and the Americans with their weapons drawn, we finally gave up. It was explained to us later that the only thing that saved us was the fact we had a bill of sale. I don't know how good this bill of sale would have been in a court of law, but it seemed to work that night, or maybe our freedom was simply a function of the extra 1000 lira we gave the old guy.

After a week chock full of such activities, we left Naples and headed for Glasgow, Scotland in something of a self-induced comatose state. Somewhere en route, Tread and I lost our bread room jobs, which was a disappointment to us both, as we thought we might be there for the duration. Instead I was assigned to a watch-keeping job on one of the ship's many turbo generators, this one in the Engineers workshop. When the ship was designed, it had been decided that the generators should be spaced throughout the ship so that all sources of electrical power were not concentrated in one place. This was sound reasoning in my opinion, though this particular generator, for whatever reason, seemed a little too well hidden.

The Engineers workshop was located somewhere below the hangar deck. First you had to find the workshop, at which point you had to find the farthest rear corner of the workshop where a hatch led down a narrow shaft to a little 14-foot compartment two decks below. In the center of this cubicle was a steam-driven turbo electric generator.

On the one bulkhead was an electrical control panel with two dials, one for wattage and one for cycles, and on another bulkhead was a phone that connected to the engine room. And that was it. There was nothing else, except a 5-gallon pail full of rags for wiping up oil and an 8-inch crescent wrench for tightening the odd steam gland. No chair, no water, nothing. You were supposed to stand down here, for four hours, with this generator screaming with such intensity that you couldn't even hear your own voice, and watch. And watch. Once an hour, you took a logbook and filled in the two readings on the bulkhead and the four temperature readings on the generator and phoned the engine room, not really knowing or caring what the person on the other end was saying. Once per watch, the Engineer would come down just to make sure you were alive and not reading or sleeping somewhere. They tried to catch you by surprise, but they didn't realize that even with the screaming of the generator the noise of their climbing down the steel ladder with it reverberating in the steel shaft was enough to alert you to their presence.

In a situation like this you had to be inventive. For instance, you dumped the waste rags out of the bucket, turned it upside down, put the rags on top and used it as a chair. If you started to get tired, you sat with your arms on you legs, leaning over, holding the crescent wrench between your thumb and forefinger. If you fell asleep, your fingers would relax and the crescent wrench would drop to the steel deck with a clatter that woke you up. You could read, but the book had to be small enough to hide when the Engineering Officer made his rounds. For anyone who believes they have a lousy, noisy, boring and claustrophobic job, chances are they've never worked the Engineers workshop generator room on the Maggie.

Speaking of which, this was to be the Maggie's last trip under the colors of the Royal Canadian Navy. Her replacement, the new carrier HMCS Bonaventure, was doing her workups in the Irish Sea at this time, and just as soon as we got her back to Halifax, the Magnificent was to be decommissioned.

Glasgow was always an interesting place to visit—there was a lot of nightlife and some great pubs—but we were only there long enough to get rid of the equipment used for launching and maintaining aircraft. They took our aviation fuel and a lot of our stores, and replaced it all with 19 F–86 Saber Jet fighter planes the RCAF had been using in Germany and didn't want to fly home. We were capable of carrying a lot more than 19 carrier-equipped aircraft, but the F–86s had fixed wings, which meant we could only get nine on the hangar deck while the other 10 had to be tied down on the flight deck. Under normal circumstances this wouldn't have been a problem, but most of the fuel and stores had come off the bottom of the ship, and parking these aircraft on the flight deck made us a little top-heavy.

While we were in port, I had a little project in mind. I caught the train to Greenock to see if the pub with the old bar-keep I'd met two years earlier was still there. It was, and he was, as though time itself had stood still in my absence. The same names were still carved into the booths, like a monument to the Canadians that had carved them years before, and the old bar-man was still behind the bar. As I walked in, he looked up and said, "Hello, Mel. Haven't seen you in a bit. It's a pint of light ale you'd be after?"

I was speechless. Either this guy had the memory to end all memories or I had made quite an impression on him—either way, it turned out to be a worthwhile trip down to Greenock, just to talk to him again.

It was a pleasant evening. Some of the old regulars I'd met on my previous visit showed up, and it was almost like old home night. Now I don't regret many things in my life—I have always held the belief that if you are looking over your shoulder at yes-terday you will be tripping over tomorrow—but I do regret never keeping in contact with some of the truly fine people I've met over the years, and these were some of them.

The day we put to sea, heading for home, we met the Bonaventure doing her workups in the Irish Sea. It reminded me of a tired old warrior, stripped of his weapons after many years of battle, meeting his fresh young replacement in the field for the first time.

I stood on the flight deck on this grey rainy day and watched the proud new HMCS Bonaventure with her bright new paint job go steaming by the tired old Maggie, with no serviceable war-planes on her flight deck and with no guns in her sponsons, hav-ing been relegated to the lowly position of a troop ship, steaming home like a freighter to await her inevitable demise in some wrecking yard in some nondescript place where she would be torn unceremoniously apart.

The next day we awoke to find ourselves facing the North Atlantic's full fury. We were steaming into a storm that was crash-ing over our bows with waves 80 to 90 feet high, and as the days went by the sea only got worse.

I was the Emergency Motor Boat Stoker on this last leg of the voyage, and as the name would suggest, I stood my watch on the boat deck beside a motor cutter, designated as the emergency sea boat, which would be launched in case of an emergency, such as a man going overboard. In my opinion, as I had looked out at the raging sea, it would have been suicide trying to launch anything in this weather. So I spent my watches sitting on a locker in my foul weather gear with the rest of the emergency boat's crew, trying ostensibly to read, but all the while thinking that being in such a little boat, in such massive seas, would be no place for a kid from Aleza Lake, BC.

With the extra weight of the F–86s on the flight deck making us top-heavy, we bounced around quite a bit, steaming 22 knots ahead while making 3 knots astern. The old Maggie was taking one hell of a beating on this her final journey. After they had stripped the ship, pieces of paper and rags and other debris left on the hangar deck that no one had bothered to pick up were washing around and plugging up the scuppers designed to let the water run out over the sides. At one point, the Maggie was hitting the waves so hard that she stove in one corner of her flight deck. It was so rough, in fact, that after a couple of days the stores men were unable to get into the refrigerators or storage lockers and we were relegated to eating boiled eggs and tinned potatoes. The crew's heads were in the bows of the ship, and every time the bow dug into the water, it would blow out the one-way scupper valve and the sea would come blasting back up through the toilet. This became know as the North Atlantic enema, not an enjoyable experience by any stretch.

After the third day we lost most of our lifeboats, and those that remained were no more than a bunch of kindling. And so, with no lifeboat to man, I stayed in my hammock most of the time. It just so happened that where I was slinging it there were these two insulated pipes with just enough room for boiled eggs and all the rum I could get my hands on. It was an exercise in safety. One of the cooks, while working in the galley awash with water, was taking a basket of eggs out of a steam chest when the ship gave a gigantic lurch and he went sliding across the galley, hit the steam table, and broke his wrist. Another night, one of the Air Force boys onboard to help our flight deck crews keep the air-craft secure, fell out of his hammock and broke his nose. The very next night he fell out again and broke his arm. For the rest of the trip he just lay in his hammock on the deck and slept as best he could, broken bones and all.

All sorts of rumours regarding our ETA into Halifax were flying around the ship. The Captain, being the glory-seeking sort he was, told us he had no idea when we were going to get back into Halifax or even if we would make it. This admission, how-ever forthright and honest, was not the tremendous boost to morale he might have envisioned it to be, especially considering the fact about 90 percent of the ship's company were already deathly ill from seasickness.

However, after four days the storm started to subside, and we ended up reaching Halifax about two days late. The sun was actu-ally shining when we arrived, and the tired old Maggie, weather-beaten and haggard, steamed into harbour with her decommis-sioning pennant flying in the breeze.

It had been announced a few days before we arrived that we west-coasters would stay onboard while the Halifax-based east-coasters would take special leave. Well this went over with us about as well as you'd expect, and so it came as no real surprise when a few of our more industrious stokers made themselves a key for the beer locker. Or when some time during the middle watch someone opened the beer locker and made off with 60 dozen beer. Upon this discovery, all leave was stopped as those in charge went in search of the wayward beer. They couldn't find any trace of it, but they opened the gangway for the east-coasters anyway, and so it was that, over the next few days, we west-coasters never went without the odd refreshment here and there.

We tied up alongside our birth to a great deal of fanfare. The jetty was lined with families of the crew, and the atmosphere, led by the band, was one of joy and happiness, all except for us west-coasters, who to a man were very bitter. Over the next two weeks, as we awaited our orders and did menial jobs around the ship, we stood our watches with a certain amount of resentment. Not to say we didn't go ashore from time to time though.

Across the harbour from Halifax is the city of Dartmouth, and every Friday night there was a dance at a place called the Mick Mac Club where Don Messer and his Islanders would play. Another stoker by the name of Al McPhee and I would head over to Dartmouth on Friday evenings and have a few drinks. Then we'd head down to the Mick Mac Club where we always managed to smuggle in a couple of 14–ounce bottles of rum, just to keep us going. It was forbidden to have alcohol on the premises, but McPhee and I, being a pair of pretty conniving characters, would slip our mickeys into our uniform pants and pull our jumpers down over top. Once we were inside, we would head into the washroom, stand on the toilet and place them in the water reservoirs mounted high on the wall. McPhee had all the angles covered.

McPhee was about 6 feet tall, well-built and good-looking, with a head of red hair and a perpetual smile on his face. But on this particular night there was a tall, well-built, good-looking, what we called Air-type from HMCS Shearwater hanging around, and McPhee and I, in our somewhat advanced state of intoxication, decided he was cramping our style. Too many of the girls were paying too much attention to him and not to us, in other words. So I told this Air-type just what McPhee was going to do to him while McPhee danced around behind me like a game boxer. The guy simply laughed, and went about his business, which was, as near as I could tell, mesmerizing every last girl in the place. And so, feeling a little deflated, not to mention defeated, we carried on with whatever we'd been doing until the dance ended and everybody was heading home.

I looked around for McPhee, but couldn't find him anywhere. Eventually I went outside where I saw a crowd standing around the sidewalk, laughing. When I was close enough to see what was going on, there was McPhee lying flat on his stomach on the sidewalk, clutching the edge of the curb and shouting, "Someone help me. I can't hold on much longer, I'm starting to slip." Everyone laughed, including Al's new buddy, the airman.

I never saw McPhee again after we returned to the west coast—his five years were up and he left the navy—although years later I got a phone call from Inuvik, in the Northwest Territories, and it was him. He was up there doing Lord only knows what and he wanted me to join him. I said to him, "Al, old buddy, there is nothing I would sooner do then join you in whatever hare-brained scheme you have going, but I'm afraid I'm now a married man with a family and can't go chasing around after you on one of your adventures." We had a good laugh and talked for a while about the old times, and that was the last I ever heard from Al McPhee.

Finally, after two long weeks of cooling our heels in Halifax, we received our orders. We were going home.

12

Upon returning to Naden, we were given 14 days special leave. Barbara had accepted my marriage proposal, and now the panic was starting to set in. "Oh my God, am I ready for this?" was the thought that kept running through my mind as June 15, 1957 rapidly approached, the day we'd set for the wedding. It wasn't the fact I thought I wasn't mature enough for such a commitment, it was the part of the marriage vows that said "until death do you part" that had me spooked. When you're 21 years old, that sort of thing seems a long way off, and rightly so.

I'd made arrangements with Barbara that upon my return from Egypt we'd make a trip up to Aleza Lake to meet my family, and after a couple of days we caught the Greyhound bus and headed north. We spent a day with my sister in Prince George, and then headed out to Aleza Lake to my mother's place.

Aleza Lake came as quite a culture shock for Barbara, what with its outdoor toilets and the only running water being the creek that ran past the house on the other side of the road, next to the railroad tracks. When you needed water, you simply grabbed the bucket, walked across the road to the creek, scooped it up and packed it back to the house. This seemed quite normal to me, even after my time served in the navy, but I was quickly informed that if I expected Barbara to move to Aleza Lake or any other place that didn't have plumbed water and indoor toilets, I was sadly mistaken.

In the Canadian Navy in those days you had to be 21 years of age before you could collect marriage allowance. Of course you could get married before that; it's just you wouldn't get paid for it. Now that I think back, I feel a little like I prostituted myself for $120 a month, which is arguably exactly what I did. In any case, on May 10, 1957 I turned 21, and one month and five days after that Barbara became Mrs. Lester Melvin McConaghy. We didn't have a big wedding; we got married in the Naval Chapel at HMCS Naden and had the reception at Barbara's parents' place. My mother came down for the wedding, and a bunch of our relatives from Vancouver showed up as well.

I must admit, Barbara got the raw end of the deal financially. Not only did she have to pay for the wedding license, she also had to pay for the first month's rent on our little one bedroom apartment. We'd picked up our furniture and groceries the day before, and on our wedding night moved in.

The wedding night wasn't what I had expected it to be. For one, Barbara's sister had conned her key out of her that day, and arriving home that night we found that Doreen and some of our so-called friends had woven toilet paper through the venetian blinds, tied pots and pans and other utensils under the bed, and left the bathtub full of water with most of our groceries floating around in it. Worse, the bed was full of thistles and rose bushes. And so we spent a good part of our wedding night not in romantic embrace, but cleaning up the apartment, a rocky start to what would be a long and successful life together.

I stayed posted to Naden until October, most of the time in the capacity of Quartermaster at the engineering school. It was a good job, and left me plenty of time to be at home with my new and, it turns out, pregnant wife. These halcyon days ended too soon however, as before long I was off to sea again, as was the way of the stoker's trade.

I joined the HMCS Antigonish on the 12th of November, 1957. The Antigonish was a Frigate with the West Coast Fourth Escort Squadron. She had started her life as a River Class Frigate, but was converted to a Prestonian Class Ocean Escort in 1956–57; we re-commissioned her on October 12, 1957. The 13 months I served on her were for the most part good and happy, due in large part to the man in charge, a Lieutenant Commander Cocks, an excellent skipper who enjoyed the loyalty of every member of the crew.

Most of our time was spent training officer cadets on what we called the "triangle run," which consisted of running down the West Coast to San Francisco, Los Angeles, Santa Barbara or San Diego—our California destination varied from trip to trip—then across the Pacific to Pearl Harbor before heading back to Esquimalt.

The next trip would be the same, but only in reverse: Pearl Harbor, wherever in California, and then home again. I think, all told, I made this trip 17 times, and after I left the navy, any time my wife mentioned the idea of heading to Hawaii, I shuddered.

In addition to the triangle run, there was the Queen Charlotte patrol and various other regular exercises warships performed in peacetime. One seemingly fruitless exercise we seemed to love to do was chase one of our own submarines around the Pacific Ocean. Although we knew approximately where it was going to be at any given time, we never seemed to be able to find the damned thing.

On a Monday morning we would race out to sea to a predetermined position off the coast of BC where we would spend countless hours steaming around the ocean with three or four other frigates trying to find a submarine that didn't want to be found, and then we would head home the following Friday afternoon. It was like a bunch of fishermen gazing out over a lake, trying to determine where just one particular fish might be. We did have one advantage over those fishermen however—our sonar—but even with that technology working in our favour we still couldn't figure out the whereabouts of that damned sub.

It wasn't until later in my naval career, when I actually served on a submarine, that I learned about the various thermo layers of the Pacific Ocean, and how a submarine could lie under a couple of these layers of differing water temperature and in effect hide from the sonar.

Upon joining the Antigonish, I was given the job of running the ship's laundry. It was a job intended not just for a seaman but for a stoker as well, there being heavy equipment involved, including a wash machine, an extractor and a dryer. Just like my wife had at home, only her washing machine had a spin-dry feature built in, and didn't require an Engineering Mechanic to run it.

This was a special duty job, which meant we didn't have to stand watches. We had every night in our bunks at sea and every night off in harbour.

One day at sea, our First Lieutenant walked into the laundry and said, "McConaghy, I'm really short of seamen on the upper deck. You think you can run the laundry by yourself?" Although I knew I could handle it easily, I stood there pondering it for a spell anyway. And all the while my partner was standing behind Lt. Cox, waving his arms to get my attention, shaking his head, "No!"

I considered the proposal a few more seconds, and then said, "Yes, sir, I think I can. But you must realize I will be working twice as hard, so I'll need some special considerations."

"I realize that. What will you need?" he asked.

"Well, first off, I'll be working almost around the clock some days, so I'd like to have a cot in the laundry so I'll be able to sleep here and not be woken up."

"Okay, what else?"

"Well, sir, I would also like to be left alone while you're making your rounds at night. In case I'm sleeping and have the door locked."

"That's fine, McConaghy. You've got it." And he turned to the seaman and said as he left, "Report to the Boson after lunch."

"McConaghy, you're a turncoat," the seaman said as he too turned to leave. "Feeding me to the wolves."

"All is fair in love and war and the pursuit of commerce!" I shouted after him.

One evening around 2000 hours, we were playing cards in the laundry and heard rounds approaching. Everyone shut up and stopped playing as the door opened and the Cox'en stuck his head in, followed by the Engineering Officer. "I didn't know you could play bridge with six people," the Cox'en said.

"Neither did I, Cox'en," I said. "This is poker."

The Engineering Officer called me out to his office where he showed me a signal recently received from Ottawa. "They are looking for six volunteers," he said. "Three from the east coast and three from the west coast, to serve on the Royal Yacht Britannia. I think you should try for it, McConaghy. It would probably be a real boost to your career."

Now at this point in my career I though I'd be in for the 20-year duration, and although I had no idea what the Britannia was, I thought, "Why not?" I didn't think I'd have a hope in hell of getting it, and as a matter of fact forgot all about it. I never even told my wife.

It wasn't until around a month later when I was summoned to the Captain's office and informed that I was to report to the Commodore's office in Naden that I started to speculate and make some inquiries. It was at this time I finally told Barbara about it.

"A worldwide cruise and a trip up the St. Lawrence Seaway," she said. "How long are you going to be gone?"

"Don't worry, I haven't got a hope in hell of getting it," I told her, still believing this was true.

Another month or so passed without any news, but then one stormy day on the North Pacific I was piped to the Cox'en's office just before up spirits: "McConaghy, you are drafted back to barracks. Something about the Royal Yacht."

I went down and got my rum and sat down with the boys to drink it. "What was that all about, McConaghy?" someone asked.

"I'm drafted."

"Drafted for what?"

"I'm going with Prince Philip on a world cruise." This last statement brought a round of laughter from my shipmates, as it deserved.

"Why would they want a rum rat like you when they have lots of ass-kissers they could send?"

"Beats me, but that's what they tell me."

We drank a lot of rum that night.

13

Barbara wasn't too happy when she found out I'd be gone for at least eight months, leaving her alone with our year-old baby. Considering the fact she was only twenty years old herself, I could certainly understand her concern. Soon enough though she realized she had married a sailor and that sailors went to sea, and she got behind me.

I thought that, being a career man planning on spending 20 years in the navy, joining the Britannia would prove an excellent career move for me. Being one of six chosen out of 20,000 for this duty, I thought an accelerated promotion would surely be in order.

On December 1, 1958 I reported to Naden and met the other two sailors going with me, Petty Officer Engineering Artificer First Class Bob Hinds and Able Seaman Cook Harry Podwasoki. Although he came equipped with that fancy title, Bob Hinds was little more than a glorified stoker, albeit a lot more senior and better trained than I. He was a very pleasant person, and we became good friends over the next nine months. Harry was a tall, slim, dark guy who really didn't say too much, but as I was to learn later, an excellent cook who took much pride in his profession.

None of us really had any idea what we were in for at this point, and there was a lot of speculation. When we finished our in-routines, we went to the Leadership School where a Lt. Commander explained where we were going, what we would be doing, and what was to be expected of us. We were also told that for the next week we'd be instructed on proper protocol, and that we'd be expected to be excellent sailors because we would be representing the Royal Canadian Navy.

The three of us looked at each other with that look that said, "What the hell have we gotten ourselves into?"

The next week consisted of lectures and detailed instruction as to how we were supposed to stand, talk and eat, and we had a lot of pictures taken. Once we finally got onboard, it became immediately apparent that no one we'd been in contact with or instructed by had any idea of just what we were in for. Then they gave us two weeks special leave.

Boxing Day, December 1958 was a day of mixed emotions for me. On the one hand I was excited because I was heading out on a new adventure, but on the other hand I was sad as I said goodbye to my young wife and our baby son. Barbara, like the brave soul she was, held me tightly as we kissed goodbye— she didn't cry or make a scene, but you knew she was very unhappy because she was very quiet. That's the way Barbara was back in the day.

After the plane took off, I looked around at Bob and Harry. They weren't looking any happier than I was, for this was a feeling every sailor in every navy gets when he leaves his loved ones to go to sea.

We switched flights in Vancouver and boarded a flight to Montreal. This being a commercial flight, it was a lot more comfortable than the last time I flew across Canada, two years before. Unfortunately, when we reached Montreal, I was reintroduced to an old and unwelcome friend, the North Star. At the time I can remember thinking, "If they'd told me I was going to be flying in one of these old dilapidated kites again, I wouldn't have volunteered." But there was another thought nagging at me as well: "We're going to have to fly across the Atlantic Ocean in this relic from World War Two. No, we're going to have to *zigzag* across it." In order to fuel up, we'd have to fly northeast to Gander, Newfoundland, then southeast to the Azores, then northeast again to Shannon, Ireland and finally, with luck, eventually make Langar, England.

In 1958 just about every country in the world had jet transports or at least turbo-props in their Air Force, and here we were flying Goony Birds. What a wretched way to start such a marvellous journey. I don't recall how many hours it took us to make the trip, but I do recall seeing the sun come up on both sides of the aircraft.

I remember sitting on the tarmac in Montreal when they were going to fire up the engines. Clutching fire extinguishers, airmen positioned themselves on each side of the aircraft, an unsettling sight for those of us onboard. The pilot fired up an engine on the other side of the aircraft without incident, and then fired up the inboard engine on my side. It sprung to life initially, and then sputtered and stopped, bursting into flames. The guy with the fire extinguisher just stood there and watched. I looked at him. He looked at the fire. I was just about to start panicking when the pilot started the engine again and it ran, blowing out the fire.

After a long painful journey replete with all the expected fuel stops and regulation cheese sandwiches, we eventually arrived at RAF Langar Air Base, somewhere in Nottinghamshire, at which point we were taken to a railroad station. It was very early in the morning and still dark when we boarded the train, and although we didn't have jetlag, we were pretty much beat. We hadn't been to bed since Christmas night.

This next leg of our journey took us from Langar to Portsmouth via British Railways. Now by this time I considered myself somewhat of an expert when it came to railway travel, but this particular trip seemed a little rougher than usual. For one, the tracks were a narrower gauge, and the train seemed to rock back and forth a lot more than I was accustomed to.

After about a half hour, they came back and told us breakfast would be served. "Great," we thought as together the six of us were herded into the dining car where we were asked if we wanted cereal or ham and "egg." We all chose ham and egg, with coffee. "Would you like white or black coffee?" the waiter asked. This stumped us, because we were accustomed to getting our coffee black and adding our own cream and sugar. The waiter informed us this was instant coffee, and that if we wanted it black it was made with hot water, while if we wanted it white it was made with hot milk.

The waiter returned with plates, knives, forks, spoons and our coffee. We sat there staring at our empty plates and drinking our less than desirable coffee until three waiters came along with large platters, one loaded with fried eggs, the second with ham, and the third with cold toast.

They proceeded down the dining car, filling our plates from their platters. First you got your egg, just the way you liked it as long as you liked it cold and fried, then your ham, and then your toast. When combined with the soot from the coal-fired locomotive, it certainly made for an interesting if unappetising breakfast. But then at least it wasn't a stale cheese sandwich.

Finally we reach our destination, Portsmouth, where a Royal Navy van met us at the station and drove us to our ship, the Royal Yacht Britannia.

She was an impressive sight as we drove up to her on that rainy, late December afternoon with her shiny dark blue hull with a gold band around it, her white super structure and her buff-coloured funnel. But on first glance, perhaps the most impressive thing about her were her three masts, the tallest being 139 feet, 3 inches from the waterline. I can still remember the excitement of standing on the jetty and marvelling at this beautiful ship, thinking to myself, "Not bad for a shy kid from a jerkwater mill town like Aleza Lake."

The Britannia was 412 feet, 3 inches long and 55 feet wide, and drew 15 feet, 7 inches of water. For a ship this size, this was a relatively shallow draught, and at sea in a good swell she would roll like an old tub if it weren't for her stabilizers, two big wings that jutted eight feet from her sides underwater. Controlled by a gyro that, when the ship started to roll, would sense it and compensate by turning one wing down and the other wing up, these stabilizers were of course retractable so as to avoid damage while tying up or manoeuvring in confined spaces.

Her 12,000 shaft horsepower could drive these 5,862 tons of ship through the water at a speed of 22.5 knots. I can remember later, while we were steaming through the Great Lakes, standing at the guardrail watching the flotillas of pleasure craft that always seemed to accompany us charging along with a bone in their teeth and a large wake trailing out behind them. When I looked over the side though, it seemed like we weren't moving that fast as the Britannia slipped silently through the water, quietly outdistancing them one after another.

One thing I noticed immediately was that forward of the funnel there were portholes in the superstructure while aft there were rectangular windows. I learned soon enough that the forward part of the ship was the working end while the aft end contained the Royal Apartments.

A photographer took our pictures as we boarded the ship, a tattered looking band of sailors to be sure. We settled into our in-routines quickly however, and this at least was familiar to us. A routine is a routine from one navy to another, regardless of the presence of Royalty.

One aspect of the Britannia that definitely surprised me was the silence of the ship. There was the regular chatter in the mess decks and the usual noise that goes with running a ship this size of course, but you never heard the ever-present Boson's whistle or the squawk of the ship's communication system so common on a warship. The crew was very friendly too, one of which took us around to address our in-routines which we completed in less than two hours. On notice boards throughout the ship, we were told, all the ship's activities were posted in the Daily Orders the night before, and it was each sailor's responsibility to read them. At the same time, some of the dos and don'ts were pointed out to us. For instance, we were never to go aft into the Royal Apartments unless we had a specific job to do, and even then only at a designated time. This one point was stressed to us over and over as the privacy of the Royal Family was to be respected at all times.

When onboard the ship, we always wore white-soled sneakers. The only time we wore shoes or boots was when we were going ashore or on watch in one of the machinery rooms. This was a preventative measure, so that the 2-inch thick teak upper deck would remain scuff-free. To keep them in pristine condition, the decks were scrubbed each and every morning, with all the work near the Royal Apartments to be performed in complete silence before 0800 so that the Royal Family would not be disturbed.

The relative informality of the crew too came as a surprise; you'd think that on the Royal Yacht everything would be by the book, when in actual fact it was quite laid back and relaxed. The Britannia was a happy ship. The fact that every crewmember was a volunteer, knew his job, and took pride in doing that job made all the difference, and in the eight months I was onboard I never heard anyone complain.

With its full seagoing complement, the Britannia carried a crew of around 300 hundred officers and men, half of which were permanent Yachtsmen while the other half were temporary. To become a permanent Yachtsman, you had to wait until one of the permanents left the ship either through promotion, through retirement or, as it was often pointed out, through death. For a permanent to get promoted, he had to wait for someone above him to leave the ship, thus vacating that position. Promotion was therefore slow for permanent Yachtsman.

For instance, there was an Able Seaman onboard by the name of Dennis Ivory who came to the Britannia from the previous Royal Yacht, the Victoria and Albert, when she was decommissioned in 1953. I don't know how old Dennis was, but he was a three-badge Able Seaman. The good conduct badges or chevrons we wore under our rate badges on our left arm were awarded for every three years of service. It was very uncommon then to see an Able Seaman in the RCN with three badges, but Dennis was what anyone would expect an old sailor to be. He had black curly hair with a full beard to match, and a tiny anchor tattooed on the lobe of one ear. He was single and lived onboard, and he did all the fancy rope work and knots that decorated the ship, especially on the aft end.

The ship was designed to be converted to a hospital ship in wartime. It was originally designed with four-man cabins and a cafeteria for the crew, but being steeped in tradition the Royal Navy would have no part of such luxuries, even on the Royal Yacht. They changed it to broadside messing and, of coarse, hammocks.

This strict adherence to the Royal Navy's Queens Rules and Regulations was never more apparent than when, later that year, we took the Queen and Prince Philip to Canada for the opening of the St. Lawrence Seaway. Even though the Canadian government was paying for the trip, dinner every Wednesday featured the same dehydrated vegetables the Royal Navy always served on that day. That seemed a little strange to me, considering it was late summer and all the fresh vegetables that were being harvested at that time of year.

As we performed our in-routines that first day, we were issued our Royal Yacht cap tallies, shoulder patches and uniforms. The uniforms weren't any different than our regular uniforms, except for the bellbottoms. The normal uniform featured navy-blue serge bells with a zipper fly, but on the Britannia the bells were made out of a material called doeskin. Also, a flap on the front buttoned across the top with five buttons, with one button on either side. You wore your jumper tucked into your pants instead of on the outside, which made for a very smart looking uniform, especially if you had the build for it. To put the bells on, you pulled them up like a normal pair of pants, then pulled the waistband around and buttoned it. Then you pulled the flap up and buttoned up the seven buttons, representing each of the seven seas. This rig was only for your number 1 uniform, worn with the gold badges. With your number 2 uniform, you wore your regular jumper with white badges instead of the red ones you wore in the regular service. But for shore leave you wore only the number 1.

The really outstanding thing about these bellbottoms was the silk bow on the back. It was made from a one-inch wide strip of black silk with a bow four inches across, with two six-inch tails that hung down the back of the waistband.

That being said, there were problems with this uniform. For instance, the ladies liked to pull on your bow to see if your pants would come off, and the occasional so-called tough guy would make fun of the cute little bow on the back of your pants. However, "Yachtees," as we Royal Yachtsmen were called, didn't fight. We simply looked down our noses with a superior look and walked quietly away. As a combat technique, it was actually quite effective in shutting these guys up, especially in a crowd.

The next day, when I reported to the engineer's office to get my workstation and steaming station, I met the Chief Stoker, Chief Petty Officer "Jock" Hogg. Old Jock was a permanent yachtsman. I later found out he'd been a young Able Seaman stoker onboard the HMS Exeter, one of the three British light cruisers that had engaged the German pocket battleship, Graph Spee, and drove her into Rio during the battle of the River Platt. The way the story was related to me, a torpedo had penetrated the boiler room without exploding, killing the Petty Officer and the other stoker on watch. According to some stories, old Jock was still maintaining steam in the boiler when the damage control party reached him, standing in seawater running over the deck plates. Quite rightly, he was very highly decorated for this.

I was assigned to the boiler room for both my workstation and my steaming station, which on the Britannia proved a pleasure. The boiler fronts were aluminum while the remainder of the equipment was painted white. The valve wheels, which opened and closed the valves, were chrome-plated, and all brass and copper was polished to a shine. The aluminum deck plates sparkled, and the bilges were painted white and spotlessly clean. Wherever there was a steam drain, or where oil might exit a steam gland, a stainless steel tray was there to catch the residue. At first appearance, it seemed as though a lot of work would be required to maintain such high standards, but in actual fact, once they were achieved, it didn't take all that much.

However, as good as the Britannia was in her mechanics and operations, she more than made up for in her culinary executions. The British have never been known for their imagination when it comes to food, and the Britannia proved no exception.

This shortcoming came to light one of the first mornings onboard, when we were served "red lead" and bacon for breakfast, this nickname for stewed tomatoes being borrowed from a paint used as a rust inhibitor. And the following Sunday morning we were served bacon and, once again, "egg." Coffee was served Sunday morning for breakfast, and that was it for the week, which, with how it was prepared and how it tasted, wasn't necessarily a bad thing. It was a concoction brewed in a large steam-heated vat. First they'd fill the vat with water, then dump in the cream and sugar, chuck in the coffee in a large cheesecloth bag, then boil it for an undisclosed length of time before sending it down to the mess decks where it would be promptly spat out.

Like the rest of us Canadians, Petty Officer Bob Hinds liked his coffee, especially during the mid-watch. He made some inquires, and learned there was coffee available for the machinery rooms, and so in the boiler room and engine room we fashioned heating coils out of quarter inch copper tubing. The coils came down from a steam drain into a coffee pot, back out the top and down into a bilge tray. The Britannia used superheated steam (1600 degrees F), so it was simply a matter of filling the pot with water, dumping in the coffee grounds, raising the pot to the steam coil and opening the drain for three seconds and you had some of the best mid-watch coffee possible, piping hot.

Word of our ingenuity quickly made its way around the ship, and soon it wasn't uncommon, during a late watch, to have the messenger from the bridge come down to one of the machinery rooms with a handful of cups.

At various times throughout the voyage, Prince Philip would come down to the boiler room and have a cup of our "mid-watch brew" as it became known. He did admit that it was good coffee, and must really have liked it, because it wasn't odd for him to show up and have a cup at any given time.

On January 7, 1959 we departed Portsmouth on a dismal, rainy day and headed for Gibraltar. The ship was a treat to sail on: the boiler room was one of the quietest I'd ever steamed in, with none of the clatter and dinginess of a normal warship. We arrived in Gibraltar on the morning of the 11th, and I went ashore with a couple of my Royal Navy messmates when the gangway opened at 1200. We performed the usual tourist routine, exploring the fortress city and the rock of Gibraltar itself. One of the hands I went ashore with had at one time been stationed there, so it was almost like having a professional guide.

The next day we went ashore later in the afternoon, and early that evening we went to a Flamenco cabaret. Flamenco dancing had always interested me, and the thing that really impressed me, besides the guitar playing, was how the dancers showed so much emotion in their dancing and yet so little in their expression. What emotion I did detect was total concentration and determination, reminding me of an athlete striving to do her absolute best.

We left Gibraltar at 0800 on the morning of the 14th of January and sailed east across the beautiful blue Mediterranean Sea, arriving in Malta on the morning of the 16th, sailing majestically into Valletta Harbour, the capital of that little fortress island. This little piece of rock that over the centuries has seen so much conflict is only 50 miles long, and yet by virtue of its location, at one time or another every major power in the world has wanted to possess it.

During World War II, this little island and its three smaller sister islands endured some of the heaviest bombing of the war. It is estimated that over 14,000 conventional bombs were dropped on it, and to honour the bravery of the Maltese people, King George IV awarded this island fortress the George Cross.

The streets of Valletta were very narrow, following the contours of the rocky terrain. Although the island isn't large, it is steeped in history, and each new twist and turn yielded another chapter from its storied past.

On the 18th of January we sailed for Port Said to begin our journey through the Suez Canal. I couldn't help but notice, as we sailed into Port Said Harbour, how the entrance of the canal had been cleared of its debris. All the wreckage of sunken ships from my visit two years earlier was gone. There was no fanfare, no waving of flags, and though I never thought about it at the time, there must have been some concern about our security. I mean it had only been three years since Britain, along with France and Israel, had invaded this country, and here we were sailing through the canal with Prince Philip onboard.

As I sit here now, reflecting over our itinerary, there is no indication that we were anywhere near Egypt on that trip. It simply states that we left Malta on the 18th of January and arrived at Aden, on the southernmost tip of Saudi Arabia, on the 26th. So maybe it was just my imagination and we weren't really there at all. Years later, when I began researching this book, I contacted an ex-RN shipmate and mentioned this missing portion of our itinerary, and he said we didn't go through the Suez. I said, "But we had to. How else do you get from the Mediterranean to the Red Sea without going through the Suez Canal?" So then he agreed we must have, but couldn't remember it.

We sailed southeast through a Red Sea as smooth as a mirror. The weather had warmed up considerably, and during our off time we sunbathed on the upper deck.

Aden is a little piece of land at the bottom of Arabia that looks like an appendix at the bottom of a stomach. The British purchased the land from some local chieftains long before it was officially proclaimed a crown colony in 1937. The surrounding area then became known as the Aden Protectorate, and in 1967 it was given back, this time to the newly formed country of Yemen. Our visit to Aden was another short one, only two days, but a few of us still managed to cross the border to a place called Crater City. It was here I first learned the value of a human life in some of these Middle Eastern countries, as at one point we were approached by a somewhat shady looking character offering to kill anyone we wanted for 10 shillings cash. And later we stumbled upon a collection of human hands in various states of decay dangling from a wire strung across a market square. These were the hands of thieves caught stealing. Justice here was swift and final.

Later, the local RAF personnel at the base challenged the ship's company to a game of basketball. The British aren't noted for their affinity for basketball, but because the game was invented in Canada it was assumed that all Canadians could play. I was the only Canadian that played that day, and don't think I lived up to their expectations.

I wasn't disappointed when we left Aden on the 28th and sailed for Vizagapatam, India in the Bay of Bengal. Two days in

Aden were enough; the surrounding countryside was depressing, though the beaches themselves were excellent. The next nine days were spent cruising through the Indian Ocean, and although we were just above the equator the weather was pleasant. The sea was calm, and again we spent a great deal of time sunbathing on our off-duty hours.

On the 14th of February 1959, we tied up alongside the dock at INS Sicard, the Indian naval training station on the outskirts of Vizagapatam, used for training recruits for the Indian Navy. It was clean and not so unlike HMCS Cornwallis where I had taken my basic training. The buildings were white-washed and tidy in the sun, and the Indian sailors were crisp and clean in the same uniforms as the British and Canadian Navy, presenting a stark contrast to what we were going to find outside the main gate.

That first evening in harbour we stayed on the base. The Indian Navy, honouring our arrival, presented us with a large banquette of traditional Indian food along with entertainment courtesy of some local dancers. It turned out to be a very lovely evening, dining on some of the most delicious East Indian food I've ever tasted, and a memory I would cling to as the next after-noon, when we went ashore, we were hit by the sight of the most abject poverty possible.

I had always thought I had grown up poor, but looking around now I knew I'd never really known what the word meant before. People were living in huts with low mud walls and thatched roofs, whole families sharing a single room. Cattle roamed the streets at will while the people around them looked like they were starving. Grown men and women, and little chil-dren in rags, begged for money and food in the village streets. Everywhere I looked there was poverty, starvation and disease.

At one point we happened upon some roadwork where men, women and children were breaking rocks into gravel with ham-mers. The men used sledgehammers while the women used smaller hammers, with the children using smaller hammers still. Their work was watched closely by some nasty looking boss-types hovering about, and I was told later these workers had to in fact pay for their jobs. If they didn't perform, there was always someone else willing to pay to take their place. Corruption, it seems, ran rampant, only adding to the considerable misery already on display.

The Indian Government at the time was keeping imports to a minimum. The only car available for purchase was a 1955 Dodge, manufactured in India using antiquated equipment purchased from Chrysler. The only clock or watch was a West Clock, also manufactured in India using equipment long considered obsolete. I learned that if you had the money and paid the right official, you could import whatever you wanted. But then considering the fact a 1955 Dodge, manufactured in India, cost about $10,000, you'd need a lot of money.

A company called Cal-Tex, co-owned by Standard of California and Texaco, operated a refinery here. Most of the key employees were from Europe and North America, and these people lived in the lap of luxury in a gated community surrounded by high stone walls. This was to keep out the snakes, I was informed, and it must have worked, because I've never heard of a cobra that could jump an 8–foot wall.

They lived in this castle with its country club, its swimming pool and its bar. They had maids to clean for them, cooks to cook for them, houseboys to wait on them and nannies to look after their children. I often wondered how these people managed to readjust to their middle class lives when they returned home to places like Nebraska and Toronto. Still, while I was there I met a family from Victoria with whom I spent quite a lot of time. I must admit I found it a welcome escape from the harsh reality waiting just beyond the gate.

One day, on one of my ventures through Vizagapatam, I noticed some little western bungalows located just outside the fence of the refinery. The doors and windows were broken, and walking through one of them I noticed how the drywall had been torn out. The floors were covered in cow dung.

Later I asked one of the people at the country club, "Why doesn't the company fix up those places for the Indian employees? Wouldn't that make sense?"

"They were actually built for them," I was told. "But the locals, they just couldn't get used to them. They wouldn't close the doors, the cows would wander in, and within six months they looked like that. The locals, they all just went back to their mud huts after that. When you've lived a certain way for centuries, see, it's difficult just to change overnight."

I didn't know what to say to that.

14

On February 14th, after eight days in Vizagapatam, we set sail for Singapore. I really can't say I was disappointed to be leaving. The rampant poverty and radical dichotomy of lifestyle were starting to bother me, not to mention the oppression and corruption.

We entered Singapore Harbour on February 22nd. The one thing all sailors look forward to when they enter a port of call is mail call, and one of the first things to come aboard is the mail from home. Writing home was a good way for sailors to help pass the time at sea, and I was no exception in this regard. Barbara and I corresponded regularly.

One hand from each mess deck would make his way to the ship's post office and wait for the postmaster to sort the mail, while the hands that weren't on watch waited impatiently below. Finally the hand would bring the mail to the mess deck where everyone listened in eager anticipation of his name being called.

This was the one time that even the most hardened sailors wore their hearts on their sleeves. As their name was called they would jump up and howl, "Yo, that's me." Some of the hands got a fistful of letters while others, if you looked around, received nothing and sat silently forsaken by themselves. One of our messmates hadn't received any mail for a month and was ready to jump ship until finally, in Singapore, he got an armful. He was almost beside himself with joy; he and his wife were very much in love and wrote each other almost every day. It seemed that the Royal Navy Postal Service, like all postal services, had managed to misplace some mail.

When I got my mail I would separate it by sender—letters from Barbara, letters from Mom, and letters from my sister

Shirley—and then by dates. The second letter from Barbara informed me we were going to have another addition to the family. This was cause for celebration of course, and everyone on the mess deck offered me their rum at tot time. By the time I'd drank all I could I was in no condition to go ashore, so I lay down on one of the mess deck benches and prepared to sleep it off. They woke me at dinnertime by tipping the bench over and rolling me onto the deck. I was sick, but happy, and stayed onboard that first night in Singapore and wrote my darling wife.

The second night, of course, I went ashore. The beauty of sailing with the Royal Navy was that someone in your mess deck had probably visited any given port you found yourself in at some point during their service. The British had bases all over the world, and the Far East was no exception, which meant I didn't have to find my own way around. It was very considerate of the Royal Navy to supply me with guides just about everywhere we went, the only exception being Panama, as this was my territory so to speak.

Singapore was a sharp contrast to Vizagapatam. It was a large, modern and very clean city, and though I'm sure there was poverty, it certainly wasn't visible to me. My guides took me to a place called the Britannia Club, not unlike the U.S.O. clubs in the States. Run by volunteers, it had a good, reasonable restaurant and a nice swimming pool. There was one big difference though. The Britannia Club had bars.

There were three bars in fact, each one seemingly better than the last. However, the British expected their men to act with dignity when confronted with alcohol, and I was sailing with the most dignified drunks you'd ever expect to meet.

The Britannia Club was two storeys with a balcony overlooking the pool at the back. Inevitably, the first thing someone would tell first-time visitors to the club was a story about some sailor having had too much to drink before trying to dive from the balcony into the pool. Not surprisingly, some of them made it and others didn't depending on who told the story and how much *they* had had to drink.

There was a distance of about eight feet from the edge of the balcony to the edge of the pool below, and throughout the night you'd see someone looking over the edge, thinking, "I could make it." Common sense prevailed that night, and everyone stayed dry, all except a little Scotsman I used to run with by the name of "Jock" Denny. But it had nothing to do with the pool unfortunately. The city of Singapore had monsoon ditches that paralleled the sidewalks. These ditches were about a foot and a half wide at the top and about three feet deep, with small plank bridges that crossed them here and there. Well old Jock must have missed a step somewhere, for he suddenly vanished as we were making our way back to the ship. We looked around and called, but he was gone. Then we heard his fine Scottish voice: "Will one of you assholes get me out of this sewer?" What followed was quite a discussion on whether we should leave him in there until the next rainfall, at which point he could float out, or go in and get him. Well, common sense prevailed again, and after a few more good laughs we pulled him out, with Jock calling us every name he could think of throughout. He ended up with some scrapes and bruises, and one arm was in a sling for a couple of weeks, but more importantly we had a really good story to tell the next day at tot time.

On February 25th we left Singapore behind, and after three days at sea steamed into Kuching, Borneo. We were only in port one night, just long enough to wave the flag and for Prince Philip to attend one of his many social functions. It's a tough job he had, and I don't say that in jest. I really did think it was a lousy job, always being in the spotlight and always having to smile and shake hands, no matter what you thought of the person you were smiling at and shaking hands with.

Being a member of the British Royal Family has to be one of the most demanding jobs in the world. The eyes of your country and the world are on you at all times, and they are not always friendly. Politicians face the same scrutiny, but when their term in office ends so does the scrutiny. The members of the British Royal Family live with it from the time they are born until the time they die. I would come to realize, in time, that even though they lived like and were treated like the Royalty they were, I was the lucky one, because I could chose my own path in life.

The next day we sailed for Sandakan, North Borneo, steaming up a wide, winding river enclosed on both sides by thick, lush jungle, arriving on the 1st of March. Sandakan is known historically for its prisoner of war camps and death marches instituted by the occupying Japanese forces during World War II, but the Sandakan I saw was a very pleasant modern city, located though it was in a jungle. Coming as I did from a forestry community, I was very interested in the logging industry that thrived in the jungle.

The primary difference, notwithstanding the types of trees they logged, was the means by which they logged them. Back in Canada we used power saws, cats and trucks to log, while here they used axes and elephants. I asked one of the loggers why they didn't use the more modern technology, and he told me they'd tried, but that the engines in the equipment would seize up, often during operation, due to the high humidity of the jungle. Such equipment would rust over a weekend, so in the end they had to stay with their traditional methods.

The second day we were in Sandakan, the locals threw a cocktail party for the crew at the cricket club. There were tennis courts located alongside the cricket pitch where they put on what was known as a "Ding-Dang" which, as near as I could tell, meant more native music and dancing. During the performance, Prince Philip and the rest of the dignitaries sat on a raised platform at one end of the tennis court, while the officers sat on chairs on either side. Surrounding the tennis court, to keep the locals from sitting on it, they'd built a three-foot fence of timber topped by barbed wire. Before leaving the ship at noon, we fortified ourselves with rum, and at the cocktail party that lasted until very late that night, we took full advantage of the open bar. Finally, to be polite, we wandered over to the tennis courts to watch what was left of the Ding-Dang.

The one thing we hadn't factored in was some local native liquor being offered up that evening. I couldn't figure out, nor have I ever figured out, what it was made from, but it was a very pleasant concoction, and I found myself quite drunk on account of it. It made our navy rum seem rather weak by comparison, and it wasn't long after its introduction to the festivities that most of the guests were up dancing with the locals, raising the Ding-Dang to a whole new level of jollity.

When my buddies and I decided it was time to return to the cocktail party, instead of walking all the way around to the gate, I decided, or rather the alcohol decided, that I should simply vault the fence. As it turned out, this was a very bad decision on the alcohol's part. Because it wasn't until I was about halfway over that I realized my hand was impaled on the barbed wire atop it.

Managing to free my hand, I in turn caught my arm, tearing open the inside of my bicep. It wasn't a bad cut, but being on the fleshy part it bled quite nicely regardless, and when my buddies came over to survey the damage I was apparently mumbling something to the effect of, "Us cowboys hate barbed wire." Picking me up, they took me back to the clubhouse where a very lovely young woman bandaged my arm, whereupon the three of us stumbled back to the ship. It was very late, or very early, when we left the cricket club, and the sky was a menacing black. Wind swept the streets over which only the occasional streetlight shone, and where there ought to have been buildings on either side only jungle greeted our drunken eyes. We'd been quite boisterous when we left the clubhouse, but now, after we'd walked about a half a mile through all that jungle, a hush fell upon the group. I don't like to think we were getting spooked, but the chatter did pick up again once we rounded a corner and saw the familiar silhouette of the Britannia up ahead. In the end I don't know how many people caught wind of this little mishap of mine that night, but the next morning when I passed the Engineering Commander in the passageway, he said, "I hope you've been staying away from that barbed wire, cowboy," and smiled as he walked away.

The next morning we left Sandakan, arriving in Hong Kong three days later, on the 6th of March. I was on duty on that first day, so I went ashore with Jock Denny the next. Jock had been stationed in this part of the world—the Far East Station, as it was known—and had agreed to show me around. I wanted to do some shopping for Barbara and Michael, and as I soon found out, if you want bargains in an oriental port, you go ashore with a Scotsman.

A couple of times I thought Jock was going to get in a fight with one of the vendors—I was embarrassed at times, but he assured me they'd be disappointed if you didn't haggle with them at least a little. I have often thought, later in life, that I could have benefited from Jock's negotiation talents and tactics.

On the way back to the ship, just outside the dockyard, Jock and I decided to stop and have a drink with the few shillings we had left. We were standing at the bar drinking our pints when an Australian airman standing next me with some of his buddies turned and looked at me. He looked at the Canada badge on my shoulder and asked me why I was wearing it.

"Well I'm Canadian," I told him.

"Well then what the hell are you doing on that limy ship?"

"I'm on detached duty from our navy for this cruise."

"Well, mate, you had just better come over here and have a few drinks with us Aussies," he said, and looking over his shoulder shouted to his mates, "Hey look here, I've found a Canuck!"

"I would love to, but I've just been shopping for my wife and son and I'm broke. And anyway I came ashore with Jock, and I should really go back with him."

"I don't recall asking you for a financial statement," he said, "and the Scotsman looks like a big boy, so he'll be all right. Besides, your ship's right over there." He pointed out the window. "He should be able to find it."

It was the custom, when in a foreign port, to return to the ship with the person you came ashore with, so that no one was left behind. Still, I asked Jock if he minded if I stayed and had a couple of drinks with the Australians.

"No, that's okay with me," Jock said. "Like he said, I can see the ship from here. I'll take your packages back with me."

Now I've run with some crazy people in my time, but I've never run with a bunch like those Australians. It soon became very clear to me that they were definitely descended from the original British convicts sent to colonize that continent.

At one point during the night, or early morning, we found ourselves on a street lined with portable food carts. You could buy just about any kind of food or souvenirs you could in the regular restaurants and shops during the day, and as the bars were shut down at this time of morning, you could also buy bootlegged beer out of the back of most of these rolling emporiums. An illegal concoction brought over from Red China, this so-called beer was called Three Lambs, and tasted more like the sewer water that ran along the little ditch between the street and the curb. I spit out my first taste, but the Australians seemed to like it, so I kept going as best I could.

Sleeping behind one of these carts, in the gutter, was a New Zealand sailor from one of their ships. His buddy lifted up his head, poured some of this terrible brew into his mouth, and said, "Okay, mate, it's time to get back to our ship."

The sailor sat bolt upright, shook his head violently and, as sober as a judge, got to his feet and helped his mate, the one who'd woken him, stumble off down the street. I thought to myself, "Whatever it is in this Three Lambs beer that can bring a man out of a drunken slumber and onto his feet, then help his buddy back to the ship, can't be all *that* bad," and had myself another drink.

It was early that morning when I returned to the ship. I had to turn to and work the forenoon watch, but seeing as we'd gone to sea, I didn't have to stand watch until the second dogwatch. I hadn't drank that much the night before—being with strangers I'd wanted to keep my wits about me—and except for being a little tired I felt pretty good, despite my lack of sleep.

There is a tradition in most navies called "crossing the line." As near as I can tell it started sometime in the 19th century, originally as a test to see if new sailors were up to the long and sometimes dangerous task of crossing the Pacific Ocean. Those who had already crossed the equator were called "Shellbacks, Sons of Neptune," and those who hadn't, "Pollywogs."

King Neptune and his court, including Her Highness Amphitricha, were among the dignitaries who attended this ceremony in the beginning. Back then the ceremony could be quite savage, and according to history more than one person died as a result, but since the introduction of human rights they were mostly just a lot of fun with some occasional mild hazing.

On that day, the 8th of March, I skipped the ceremony for some time in the funnel. On most ships, the funnel served one purpose: to carry the exhaust from the boilers to the atmosphere. The funnel on the Britannia, however, came with large forced-draft fans and a system that washed the exhaust, preventing any soot from discharging into the atmosphere. The last thing they wanted was for the members of the Royal Family to be sun-bathing on the upper deck with soot from the boilers drifting down on them.

All this machinery had to be kept clean and rust-free, although very few people actually took the time to venture up into it. When at sea, when we weren't actually on watch, we spent the forenoon watch working in our designated workspaces. My workspace, of course, was the boiler room, and it didn't take long for me to realize the funnel, being part of the boiler room, was a good spot to disappear inside. Although it was very hot in the tropics, it was a good place to go for a little time alone on a crowded ship.

The heat in the funnel rarely bothered me, as I could work at my own pace, but when it did bother me, I simply opened the hatch at the top, three decks up. Opening the hatch and standing with your head and chest in the breeze was an excellent way to get a break from the heat, and also to have a good look around. And with no one else willing to endure the heat inside the funnel, I'd spend hours, when I was so inclined, taking in the fresh air and soaking in the visual panorama. As ironic as it seems, this hot, noisy space was my escape at sea. Even with the hum of the large electric motors, the fans and the noise from the boiler room, it was peaceful up there. As there was nothing technical to do my mind could wander, and I'd lose myself in fantasies for hours on end, just scraping, chipping rust and painting all day. Of course the rest of the boiler room hands thought I was crazy. "Crazy damned Canuck," was the actual expression they used, if I remember correctly.

After leaving Hong Kong, we started island hopping through the Gilbert, Elise and Solomon Islands. Our itinerary looked liked this:

ARRIVED	LOCATION	DEPARTED
18th March	Gizo	18th March
19th March	Honiara	19th March
20th March	Malaita	20th March
22nd March	Graciosa Bay	22nd March
25th March	Tarawa	27th March

We went ashore on Tarawa for a day, a nice tropical island to walk around on despite all the evidence of war on display. Old tanks and guns, abandoned by all but their accelerating rust, were being slowly swallowed up the jungle at every turn. It was depressing, in a way.

Ocean Island was a small island made up almost completely of Bauxite, a material used to smelt aluminum. Over the years the Australians mined it steadily for just this purpose, and I have often wondered how much of the island was left when they finished. This small inhospitable pile of rock sat out in the middle of the Pacific Ocean with nothing around it for as far as the eye could see. There was no harbour, just a wharf sticking out into the ocean, and we were told that it was susceptible to storms that could blow up at a moment's notice. For this reason, then, it was decided we'd anchor offshore. That way, if a storm did come up, the ship could get to deep water in a hurry. One only need look at the Bauxite freighter lying rusted on the beach to know how sound a decision this was.

The manager of the island's Bauxite plant had invited Prince Philip and the crew ashore for a cocktail party, and though only half the crew would be able to attend, I just happened to be one of them. We spent a very pleasant afternoon touring the island, followed by the requisite afternoon drinks.

After Ocean Island, we sailed for Christmas Island where the British tested their atomic bombs. The entire native population had been removed from the island so that they could blow it up to their hearts' content. Then, when things cooled down, they came back and blew it up all over again.

When we arrived, I don't recall if they'd blown it up yet, or were just getting ready to blow it up. Regardless, there were 2700 men and 3 women on the island apparently, most if not all of whom were military personal. I never did see any of the women. The only place we were allowed to go while ashore was the wet canteen. I'm sure they sold things besides beer there, though I sure didn't see any.

These poor souls stationed on this little island, all 2703 of them, with no other place to go and nothing else to do, gathered at the canteen and drank beer all day. The place was massive—it looked like a hockey arena in there—except all available ice was being used to cool the beer.

There were tables in the center with five or six bars around the outside. No one bought "a beer"—they bought them by the case of 24, and as the evening wore on the tables, those few still standing, would be stacked with empties. There were people passed out, some on top of the tables with the empties and others under the tables with the empties. Everywhere you looked, men were fighting one another, but no matter; here on Christmas Island this was deemed acceptable human behaviour. Drinking and fighting, it seemed, was all these men had to do out here.

And so it was that, on the 5th of April 1959, we left this tropical paradise to its custodians so that they could blow it up once again, all to a chorus of barfing, brawling and the rattle of empty beer cans.

After almost two weeks at sea we tied up in Balboa, Panama. Now we were back in my part of the world, and for the one day we were there it was my turn to show the Brits around. The following day, the 20th of April, we sailed through the Panama Canal to Colon, and then to Nassau for two days. The people of Nassau loved the British, mainly because they were mostly British themselves, but they didn't like the Canadians much, mainly because our navy sailed into Nassau quite a lot. They thought we were a bunch of colonials and barbarians.

Bermuda was our last port of call, though only for a day before we were once again underway, sailing across the Atlantic. Channel fever was running high the closer we got to Portsmouth, and most of the crew sat up at night talking about their families and home. But for me, with all this talk of home and knowing it would be months before I'd see mine, it was a sad time.

We arrived back in our homeport of Portsmouth on May the 2nd, having travelled a total of 24,537 sea miles on a voyage that lasted 120 days. Of these 120 days, we were underway for 107 of them, leaving only 13 days spent ashore.

I can remember the excitement and fanfare as we tied up that day. The band was playing, wives and girlfriends were crying, children were dancing, and it seemed like everyone onboard was running around happy to be home. Everyone but me, that is.

It wasn't until we were secured to the jetty and the ship was shut down that I realized I wasn't the only one feeling alone that day. In addition to the other five Canadians, part of the regular crew had to stay onboard to watch over the ship. A feeling of sorrow followed these individuals wherever they went. It didn't help that, prior to our arrival in Portsmouth, it had been announced that the crew was to be granted two weeks' leave for the month we'd be in harbour getting the ship ready for the cruise up the St. Lawrence Seaway. The Starboard Watch, of which I was a part, would get the first two weeks, while the Port Watch would get the last two weeks.

Having a young family at home, and not having the financial resources to spend two weeks ashore in England, I decided to take onboard leave. This meant I'd have to turn to and work every morning, leaving the rest of the day to spend as I wished.

I'd made many friends amongst the crew, but these men had their own families ashore, and the last thing I wanted to do was tag along with them. I talked to the rest of the Canadians and most of them were doing the same as I.

Onboard ship, you live in the same mess deck as the people you work with, but if you're not on the same watch or work in the same work space, you might not see them for days. The Chief Petty Officers and Petty Officers had their own messes, just as the seamen and stokers did, so I didn't see the rest of the Canadians on a regular basis.

I was all set to spend the next month onboard the ship when Leading storesman, Des Hawes, a Brit I'd talked too on several occasions of late, came up to me and said, "I understand you're taking ship-board leave."

"Yes, I'm afraid so," I said. "I really don't think I can afford to live ashore for two weeks."

"I talked to my wife last night and told her about you, and we decided you should come stay with us," he said. "We have plenty of room, and with Molly and I working during the day you can do what you want."

"I don't think so, Des. You two should have your own time."

"I really don't think you have a choice," he said. "When Molly makes up her mind, it's final. Go on now. I'll wait for you to get some gear together and then we'll go home."

I spent the next ten days with two of the warmest, most wonderful people I have ever met. When I walked into their home that evening and met Molly, it was as though I had just come home. They treated me like one of the family my entire stay, and that's why one of the biggest regrets I have is the fact that, through my own stupidity or negligence or both, I've lost track of so many good people over the years. In my defence I can only say that, as you get tied up in your own life, chasing dreams and raising a family, you lose sight of some of the wonderful people you've met along the way. Then, when you get older and begin to look back on the past and the people you met, became friends with and eventually lost track of, you have regrets. When I started doing the research for this book, I was able to get in contact with one of my old shipmates through a letter to the editor of the Navy News. When I asked if he could find out what happened to Des, I was informed he had passed away. My old shipmate also got me Molly's address, and I wrote her, but at this time I still haven't received a reply. Too much time has passed perhaps.

When I finished my leave and returned to the ship, it was in dry-dock for repairs. A ship in dry-dock is nothing if not depressing—almost like a whale lying dormant on the beach—and the Britannia was no exception. Dockyard "maties," the civilian dockyard workers, crawled over the ship's corpse like parasites with their welding cables, airlines and an assortment of other hoses and cables the maties seemed intent on stringing from one end of the ship to the other. Our ship was a mess, and the knowledge that when these people had finished their work she would be her old self again, all shiny and bright, did little to assuage this initial feeling of disgust.

In addition to other various repairs, the Britannia's hull was sanded and repainted, and a rubbing strake, a series of long 12–inch-square timbers fastened end to end from bow the stern, was installed along the waterline to protect the ship from the locks she was about to traverse. When all was said and done she looked good, I had to admit, and so it was that, on the 6th of June 1959, we sailed for Canada with the old ship shining like a new dime, ready for her appointment with history, the official opening of the St. Lawrence Seaway. The eyes of two nations would be continually upon her once we reached Sept Isles, Quebec eight days later. From that point on we sailed inland night and day, deep into the heart of the continent.

Queen Elizabeth and Prince Philip didn't make the voyage across the Atlantic with us; they joined the ship in Sept Isles where we took on some of the Canadian personnel helping to coordinate their visit to Canada. If I seem vague with regards to these people and their duties, it's because they were part of the Royal Staff and, as I explained earlier, if you didn't have a job that required you to go aft, you didn't go.

I never really thought about it at the time, but from this point on the Royal Household staff, including the Royal cooks and stewards and everyone else directly connected with the aft end of the ship, would be working nonstop, ensuring the official dinners onboard and ashore went off without a hitch. Meanwhile, my biggest concern was to help keep the boiler going. Back in Portsmouth I had been assigned watch-keeping duty, which meant that another stoker and I would stand watch-on, watch-off for 24 hours, at which point the other side of the watch would take it for a day.

The Britannia, whenever she was away from her homeport of Portsmouth, was always independent of any connections to shore. She always maintained steam in at least one boiler, generating her own power, and was capable of firing up and going to sea within an hour. In this way, in case of an emergency, the Royals and their ship could be whisked away to safety.

At 2200 hours on the 20th of June we left Sept Isle, arriving at Gaspe at 1000 hours the following morning only to sail again at 1300 hours. In fact, over the next 17 days, we barnstormed just about every town and city along the Gaspe Peninsula, often hitting two and three towns in the same day. Our schedule looked like this:

ARRIVED	LOCATION	DEPARTED
0930 SUN, 14 June	Sept Isle	2200 Sat, 20 June
1000 Sun, 21 June	Gaspe	1300 Sun, 21 June
0930 Mon, 22 June	Tadoussac	0930 Mon, 22 June
1430 Mon, 22 June	Port Alfred	1900 Mon, 22 June
2330 Mon, 22 June	Tadousa	2330 Mon, 22 June
1000 Tues, 23 June	Quebec	0230 Wed, 24 June
1000 Wed, 24 June	Trois Rivieres	1100 Wed, 24 June
1800 Wed, 24 June	Montreal	0930 Fri, 26 June

Finally, on the 27th of June, we ceremoniously opened the St. Lawrence Seaway. I was on the forenoon watch as the ship steamed majestically through the first lock with the Queen, Prince Philip, President Eisenhower, Prime Minister Diefenbaker and hundreds of other dignitaries amassed on the aft end of the ship.

Knowing my schedule ahead of time, I knew I'd be on watch that morning. And knowing this event would be nationally televised, I'd already written my wife, telling her to be watching as the ship started to move through the Seaway. I told her to watch for a little puff of smoke from the funnel.

Now while making smoke was taboo on any naval ship, on the Royal Yacht it was a cardinal sin. "Still," I thought, "what the hell, it'll give Barbara something to talk about." So when the engine room telegraphs repeater in the boiler room rang down "Slow Ahead" and I knew we were on our way and that all eyes would be on the aft end of the ship, I made my move.

Each boiler contained five fires, and as the demand for more steam increased, additional fires were lit. And each fire had a nozzle through which the oil was injected into the boiler. Now if you didn't open the surrounding damper when you lit a fire, you made smoke, so after I lit the fire and opened the damper, I gave the latter a little tweak so that for a split second smoke was visible.

The Stoker Petty Officer, a tough blonde Welshman by the name of Taf Rayworth, almost lost his mind, ranting and raving about it for a good fifteen minutes. We waited for the inevitable phone call from the bridge, but it never came. In the meantime, Taf explained to me, in no uncertain terms, that if he got in trouble over my little trick I could expect a good licking courtesy of himself, and I had no doubt he could do it. I assured him if anything was said I would take full responsibility. This seemed to calm him down a little, but he was still very upset with me.

I'd told my watch-keeping opposite, Bunny Warren, about my little plot beforehand. He hadn't believed I would actually go through with it, but then he saw it on TV and just about flipped. He came running down to the boiler-room, as he put it, "To watch the shit hit the fan."

But nothing happened. In the immediate aftermath I didn't hear a word about it, except from my wife, who seemed suitably impressed. It's not difficult to imagine what would have happened had some senior officer seen it, but I guess everybody was too busy watching the ceremony to have noticed, which was my plan all along. Some time later, when the Chief Stoker got wind of it through word-of-mouth, he gave me a lecture on making smoke, but that's as far as it went.

15

ARRIVED	LOCATION	DEPARTED
2230 Sat, 27th	Brockville	1000 Sun, 28th
1630 Sun, 28th	Kingston	1900 Wed, 28th
1000 Mon, 29th	Toronto	0700 Wed, 1st July

I remember Toronto vividly. You simply don't forget an experience like that. We tied up at the dock with bleachers erected on either side facing the ship in a U shape. Floodlights lit up the entire area at night, and the bleachers were almost always full. Our first day in harbour, Bunny and I were off duty at 1200, so we went ashore. As soon as we cleared the barriers that kept the crowds from getting too close to the ship, though, we were mobbed.

Posing for pictures, signing autographs, holding babies, and receiving countless offers to go out to dinner or any other place in town, it took us about an hour to clear the bleachers and get on our way. Even then, it wasn't long before we were approached by some enthusiastic locals eager to take us to their big beautiful home where we enjoyed a barbeque that lasted until early morning. When they finally took us back to the ship, we had to fight our way through the crowd. It was the same in every port, all the way along the St. Lawrence. These people seemed to think *we* were the Royalty, an obviously misguided notion I didn't bother to correct. I don't think I paid for a drink that entire trip.

After my morning watch on July 1st, I went in front of the Captain, Vice-Admiral P. Dawnay, to be promoted to Leading Seaman Engineering Mechanic, a move I considered long overdue. Later I was told that, to lose my rate, I would have to go in front of an officer equal in rank to he who'd promoted me. I don't really know if this was true, but later in my navy career, when I became disillusioned and wanted out, I pushed this rule to its limits. As for now though, I was happy with my new promotion, and so on we went.

ARRIVED	LOCATION	DEPARTED
0930 Wed, 1st July	Port Weller	0930 Wed, 1st July
1930 Wed, 1st July	Port Colborne	1930 Wed, 1st July
1100 Thur, 2nd July	Windsor	1445 Fri, 3rd July
2100 Fri, 3rd July	Sarnia	2200 Fri, 3rd July
1400 Sat, 4th July	Pentaguishine	1430 Sat, 4th July
1900 Sat, 4th July	Parry Sound	2200 Sat, 4th July
1000 Mon, 6th July	Chicago	2300 Mon, 6th July
1200 Wed, 8th July	Sault St. Marie	1600 Wed, 8th July

On the 8th of July I was called into the office for another pleasant little surprise. Having not forgotten Borneo, the Commander of the Engineering Division said with a smile on his face, "Cowboy, as you know, the Queen will be leaving the ship until the 31st of July. We are giving all you Canadians leave until we get back to Shediac on the 27th. Have a good leave, and we'll see you then."

"Uh, okay."

He clearly didn't realize that even after travelling almost halfway crossed North America on a seagoing ship, I was still 1553 miles from home. "How the hell am I going to get there and back on a sailor's pay?" I wondered. "Oh well, I guess I'll just have to hitch-hike and worry about getting back to the ship when the time comes." And so the next day, with an attaché case containing little more than some clean underwear and a shaving kit, I left the ship and began my cross-Canada trek, but not before phoning a very surprised and pregnant Barbara, telling her I'd be home in three days, give or take.

I hit the TransCanada Highway and headed west, employing my thumb the entire way. I really can't remember how many rides I got, but I travelled night and day, sleeping in snatches when and where I could. However, I do remember the last ride. I was in Calgary, and the gentleman who picked me up was going to Nanaimo, but after he found out what I was doing, with my help he decided to drive straight through and detour to Victoria. He even paid my fare on the ferry and dropped me off at my doorstep. The kindness of strangers has never ceased to amaze me, and for the road-weary traveller I can only hope it continues to this day.

After all the hellos and embraces, Barbara, being a very practical woman, said, "When do you have to be back?"

"On the 27th."

"The *27th*," she said. "How are you going to do that?"

"Don't worry your pretty head about it," I told her. "I'll figure that out when the time comes."

I spent a very wonderful six days at home, although Michael, who was about a year and a half old at the time, had no idea who this strange man sleeping with his mother was. I got the idea early on he really didn't like sharing his mother's attention with me.

Still, as enjoyable as this stint at home was, the thought that I had to return to the ship eventually plagued me continuously. I finally decided I'd get back the same way I'd arrived, by thumb and the grace of strangers. Barbara thought I was crazy, but I told her I really didn't have any other option. And so it was that, on the morning of the 20th, a friend drove me out to the ferry terminal where, after I paid for my ticket, I headed east with 15 dollars in my pocket and the token clean underwear in my attaché case. I had seven days to hitch-hike across North America and catch my ship.

I'd planned to cross into the States as soon as possible to take advantage of their freeways, and once I did I travelled 24 hours a day nonstop. I was lucky for the most part, and found my way into the company of several good drivers one after another, making good time until I hit a little nondescript town in the northern part of South Dakota, as far east as my ride at the time was going.

By this time I needed a shave and a change of underwear anyway, so with about five dollars left in my pocket I tried my luck at a little motel. I explained my situation to the woman running the place, and she gave me a room to shower, shave and get changed in. After I got cleaned up though, I couldn't resist lying down on the bed. I lay there a couple of minutes, until I realized if I didn't get up I might just be there a very long time.

I got up, finished dressing and went to the office where the woman told me to head next door to the restaurant and have breakfast on her. I objected vigorously, but she won out in the end, and as a result I enjoyed my first hot meal since leaving home. The old round rig, as my sailor suit was called, really appealed to some people's better natures on the road. Besides, you could wear them for days and with a little brushing they still looked good.

I got back on the highway. Unfortunately, sometime while I was asleep, one of my previous rides had turned off the freeway without dropping me off first, and now I was on what amounted to a secondary road. Thankfully an old red pickup stopped for me after about an hour, and I asked the driver if he was heading to the next town.

"Yup," he said, and that was the only thing he said for about an hour, at which point he announced, "This is where I turn off." He pointed to a dirt road heading off to the right.

I looked around. We were in the middle of nowhere. Then I looked at the driver and he shrugged, at which point I got out of his pickup thinking of all the things I'd like to call him. But biting my tongue, I stood there on the side of the road, silently cursing both him and myself. I looked to the north where there were some foothills about ten miles away. I looked east and then west and all I could see was the road disappearing into miles and miles of barren landscape. Behind me I could see the cloud of dust the pickup was stirring up as it rattled off down the road.

I started walking east, looking back every now and then to find nothing but emptiness. This was the start of a routine that went on well into the evening. The sound of my footsteps kept me company for a time, but after many miles even their dialogue seemed to fade into the darkness all around me. Finally I saw a light coming from the west, and my heart began to race. "I hope they pick me up," I thought. I waited and waited, but as the light drew closer and I could hear it coming I thought, "There's something wrong here." There were now two lights, but one was above the other and the top light was swinging from side to side. "Oh My God, it's a train," I said out loud. Turns out there was a set of railroad tracks about a mile north of the road.

By now it was completely dark, and I stood there on the side of the road feeling more alone and depressed than I ever had in my life. I tried to cheer myself with the idea that someone would surely come along eventually, if only to find my bones scattered along the asphalt. Maybe even the guy who'd dropped me off out here in the first place.

I sat down on my attaché case about ready to cry when I heard a rumbling sound approaching from the west. Eventually I saw two lights, this time side by side, and so I stood up, picked up my attaché case and waited as they bore down on me. "This one won't get by me," I thought, preparing to throw myself in front of whatever it was. As it drew closer I thought I could tell it was a truck, and as it went flying by me I almost collapsed in anguish at the sight of an empty car transport. Suddenly, though, the brake lights came on and the tires smoked as the vehicle came to a quick and shuddering halt.

By this time it was about a hundred yards down the road from me, so I ran as fast as I could, fearing the driver might drive off on me.

When I got to the cab, reached up and opened the door, the driver looked at me as though he was seeing a ghost. "Are you real?" he asked as I climbed inside.

"What do you mean, am I real?"

"I'm driving along in the dark, in the desert, and all of a sudden I see what looks like a sailor standing on the side of the road. Don't you think I'd be a little surprised? By the way, what kind of sailor are you anyway? I've never seen a uniform like that before."

I told him who I was and what I was doing, a story I'd told and would continue to tell many times throughout this little journey.

"That's interesting," he said, "I was in the US Navy myself at one time. I got out when I finished my hitch and now I'm doing this here." He smiled wistfully a moment, and then after a few moments asked me, "By the way, you wouldn't by any chance be able to drive this thing, would you?"

"Sure, I've driven truck before. Mostly in the bush though, hauling lumber and logs in British Columbia."

"Hey, that's great," he said. "I got sidetracked in a tavern all day yesterday, and now I'm running a day behind. If you could drive until daylight so I could get a little sleep, I'll take you as far as I can and get you back on the Interstate."

Andy, as his name turned out to be, moved over to the passenger seat as I walked around the front of the truck and got behind the wheel. I sat there a few minutes, acquainting myself with the dashboard and all its various knobs and buttons, and when I finally felt comfortable, put the rig in gear, released the brakes and pulled out onto the highway. With each shift up through the gears Andy nodded his approval, and soon he grabbed a cushion from between the seats and jammed it back between the side window and the seat back, settling in for the long night ahead. In only a matter of minutes he was sound sleep.

I drove through the night, bypassing a couple of small towns. I considered stopping for a cup of coffee in one of them, but was afraid the change in the rhythm of the truck would wake Andy up. I drove us out of the desert, and when it started to get light I was beginning to get tired, so I stopped.

Andy woke up, took the wheel, and drove a few miles farther up the road to a small town where he stopped and bought me breakfast. When we got rolling again I sat back in the passenger seat and fell into a deep sleep, and when he finally woke me up, around noon, I could see we were back on a freeway again. After about an hour he turned off the freeway and told me this was as far east as he was going. We stopped at a truck stop, he bought me lunch, and we said our goodbyes.

It's strange that in the time we spent together, even though one of us was almost always sleeping, Andy and I seemed to become friends. We exchanged addresses, but for whatever reason never got in touch with each other. Life is strange that way.

Day and night blended together as I caught ride after ride, some short and others long. I remember standing on the side of the road very early on Sunday morning. Traffic was almost non-existent when a new 1959 Ford Galaxy came flying up, screaming to a stop right in front of me.

The driver, a young man, said, "I hope you don't mind going fast because I have to get home in time for church. My dad bought me this car with the stipulation I be at church every Sunday morning." I said no problem, and as we went flying off down the freeway at astronomical speed, I was thinking to myself, "On the odd chance I survive this ride, maybe I'll take the time to go to church with him and give thanks I'm still alive."

A few short rides later, I found myself in the presence of a very large black man with an equally large wife and an even larger brother-in-law. The assured me they'd drop me off on the freeway outside Chicago so I could continue my journey east.

They didn't drop me off on the freeway outside Chicago. They dropped me of in the middle of South Chicago. When I got out of the car and looked around, I couldn't see a white face anywhere; they were all black and they were looking at me, menacingly. I was petrified. In fact, I was standing so still the pigeons were starting to circle me. Finally a police car pulled up and lowered its window. "What the hell are you doing in this part of town, white boy?"

"I have no idea, sir. I'm hitchhiking to the east coast and the last ride I got dropped me off here."

"Well you'd better get your little white ass in the car before someone has you for dinner."

I jumped in the back of the patrol car, and the two police officers drove me out to the freeway. They weren't very nice admittedly, but to me they were saints just the same.

The next ride I got was courtesy of a young couple from Manitoba heading for Nova Scotia. Having planned on stopping for the night, after hearing my story they decided to drive straight through, taking me back to my ship in Shediac, reassuring my faith in humanity.

The next evening, at 1900 hours, I climbed up the gangway of my ship officially eight hours adrift, but no one said a thing. After showering, I found my hammock and hit the rack. The next morning they almost had to roll me out of my hammock to wake me up. Later, when I went to the Engineers office, the Commander met me in the passageway. He stopped, looked at me with a funny expression, and said at length, "What are you doing back here, cowboy?"

"My leave expired, sir. As it was I was eight hours adrift."

"We didn't expect you back. We were going to send your orders and documents to you at your home."

At that I turned away muttering to myself, shaking my head in disbelief. It sure would have been nice had someone informed me of that sometime prior to my continent-traversing odyssey.

The next day, the 28th of July, we set sail, and after spending only a few hours in Charlottetown, Cheticamp Approaches, Sydney and Halifax, we headed east into the Atlantic Ocean, back to the British Isles. Originally it had been planed that the Queen would stay onboard for the trip back to the British Isles, visiting the Shetlands and Orkneys before disembarking at Aberdeen, Scotland. This plan was changed however when they found out she was pregnant.

I wonder if this was planned, or whether it was one of those romantic summer nights on our trip up the Great Lakes that Prince Philip slipped across the dining room to her bedroom and in the heat of passion they forgot their birth control. It didn't matter to me at the time; it meant I'd be going home a couple of weeks early. In fact it was only a matter of days after we reached England that our travel orders came through.

The trip home was a repeat, in reverse, of the trip over. So we took another ride on British Railways to the air base at Langar where we were told to wait for our flight home, but of course we were bumped off one flight after another by some superior officers.

Fortunately there was a Sergeants Mess right across the street where we could eat and have a drink. We sat around the mess all that day and the next—at one point we were told we'd be leaving "that afternoon," and then in turn informed we'd been bumped again. By the third day we were sitting in the mess having drinks first thing in the morning and drunk by the time early afternoon set in. Around three in the afternoon we were well into it with a group of airmen when another airman came rushing into the mess, looked around, saw us and shouted, "Petty Officer Hinds, Leading Seaman McConaghy and Corporal Jones. Have your kit ready and out in front of the barracks in fifteen minutes. You're flying out."

A mad scramble ensued as we stumbled across the street and grabbed our gear. A vehicle was waiting to drive us out to our plane, and the driver appeared mighty impatient. We made it to the airfield in record time, but when I saw the aircraft I stopped dead in my tracks. It was another North Star.

I was pleasantly surprised to see it contained about ten rows of double seats, but when I went to sit in one of them the steward told me I'd have to sit in the canvas seats. The good seats were for higher ranks of course.

We lower ranks sat in our lowly sling backs as the old goony bird taxied out to the end of the runway and started to rev up her engines. And, as if to add to our dismay, one was running rough. The captain got on the intercom and told us we had a bad carburetor on one engine and that they'd have to change it. He also told us to keep our seats as it would only take the ground crew a couple of minutes to change it.

There I was, sitting awkwardly in my seat and gazing out the window, when I saw the ground crew pushing some portable steps out to our plane to start changing the carburetor. And that was when I realized these were the same guys we'd been drinking with in the mess an hour before.

I looked at Jones. Jones looked at me. Then I looked forward to Bob, sitting in his plush comfortable seat, and he turned and looked at me, shrugged his shoulders, and tightened his seatbelt against whatever dangers lay ahead.

Despite the ground crew's inebriation, and our apprehension, we finally got off the ground and flew to Shannon, Ireland where we refuelled before heading over to the Azores to refuel again and get fed. It must have been around four in the morning, after a nice hot breakfast at the American airbase, when we boarded the North Star and taxied out to the end of the runway. Once there at the end, though, we stopped. All three of us looked at one another again.

"This is the Captain," came the expected voice over the intercom. "Our artificial horizon is malfunctioning, and so we'll have to stay here until they fly another one out from Montreal."

"The artificial horizon," Jones said. "Isn't that the thing that tells him if he's flying upside down or not? Can't he just set a cup of this lousy coffee on the dash? That'll tell him which way is up."

We all laughed. Still, there was nothing we could do, and so we exited the aircraft as we were instructed to. They assigned us beds in one of the barracks, and there we waited. Bob, being a Petty Officer, was of course assigned to a different barracks while Jones and I were in the same one. There were slot machines everywhere, even in the washrooms. In fact, everywhere you turned there were slot machines. This place made Las Vegas look like a quiet church community.

When on Foreign Service, you are entitled to one forty-ounce bottle of duty-free liquor a month. Jones had a couple in his kit bag, and I just happened to have one as well. We were frustrated and, with nothing else to do, decided to open one. After all, what harm could one quick drink do? And so it was that by dinnertime that evening we'd polished off two bottles and made a considerable dent in the third. That was when we decided to go to the Chiefs and Petty Officers Mess for dinner. Although we didn't have the required rank to get in, for some inexplicable reason they let us anyway.

We were feeling pretty good, and it wasn't long before I got on one of the ubiquitous slot machines and won $200. Well that was equivalent to a month's pay at the time, so to celebrate we decided to have some more to drink.

This would have not been a problem under normal circumstances, but behind the bar in the Chiefs and Petty Officers Mess in the Azores was a very large mirror. And above this very large mirror was a very large stuffed moose head. Now you take a boy from Aleza Lake, where the moose outnumber the people, and show him a moose head, and he is going to want to show everybody how to hunt moose. And that is exactly what I did.

According to the story I was told the next morning by my new buddy Jones, the boy from Aleza Lake crouched down in front of the bar telling his audience, "You have to sneak up on them, see, because if they see or hear you, they'll run. And if they run, you get tough meat." He crept along in front the bar with a shot glass in his hand, and when he thought he was in front of his quarry, jumped up and shot, BANG!

"Damn, I shot too low," I said as the glass from the mirror crashed to the floor, taking with it four or five good bottles of bourbon. They took all that remained of my winnings from the slots away from me—for damages apparently—and threw me out unceremoniously, banning me from their club forever. Big deal, I told them. I wouldn't want to return to their lousy bar anyway.

Around noon the next day, as we flew away from this evil island with the four big Rolls Royce engines thundering all around my fragile head, I looked for some place to lay it down. Towards the back of the aircraft I found stretchers rolled up and strapped, about eye level, to the side of the fuselage. When I undid the straps, the stretcher rolled down to hang on straps from the ceiling. I asked the steward if I could use one of them.

"Okay," he said. "Just so long as you put it back the way you found it afterwards."

"No problem," I told him, and climbed in and fell fast asleep.

When I woke up, my head felt like it was going to explode and I was having trouble breathing. "I'm going to die," I thought as I rolled over from the bulkhead about ready to cry for help. This was when I noticed that everyone else on the aircraft had their oxygen masks on.

It seemed that, while I was trying to sleep off my hangover, the pilot had run into a weather front, and instead of flying through it he'd decided to climb over it. In the meantime, the steward was checking to make sure everyone had their oxygen masks on. And seeing mine hanging down, since I was lying with my back to the isle, he assumed I was good to go.

The remainder of the flight was much less eventful.

16

The morning after I returned home to my lovely wife and a very suspicious 18–month-old son, I reported once again to HMCS Naden. As I walked around the base doing my in-routine wearing the Royal Yacht uniform, I received some very strange looks. When I finished my routine, I was given thirty days leave to see my family, which was much appreciated as I wanted to get to know my son.

On September 10, 1959 our daughter Karen was born, and I was thankful to be there. I spent a very happy thirty days with my family—Michael learned a new word, Daddy, Karen was beautiful, and my lovely wife was happy to have me home, even though I could tell she was thinking in the back of her mind: "What next?"

What next indeed. When my leave was up, I reported back to Naden to find out what they were going to do with me. I was actually hoping I might get drafted ashore for a change. Except for seven months in 1957 I had been almost exclusively at sea, and I thought that maybe I might be in line for a shore posting. No such luck however, as on the 24th of September, a mere twenty-one days after Karen was born, I was sent back to sea—sort of. I say sort of because I was drafted to the HMCS Oriole, and the Oriole was not your average warship. She was like the old Cedarwood, an oceangoing oddity, only with a great deal more class. A mere 102 feet from the end of the bowsprit to the stern, she was a Marconi-rigged ketch used to train officer cadets from HMCS Venture, the Naval College in Victoria. A ketch has two masts, the main mast forward and the mizzenmast aft.

Launched on the Great Lakes in 1921, the Oriole was the most advanced design for a sailboat at the time. During World War

II she was on loan to the Navy League of Canada, training Sea Cadets on the Great Lakes, and afterwards she spent some time on the east coast. In 1954 she switched coasts to train Venture cadets, and all this time she was being leased for a whopping one dollar a year. In 1957 she was bought and commissioned by the Canadian Navy, by which time she was the oldest and longest serving ship in the RCN.

As far as postings went, there couldn't have been a better one. People would give up a month's pay to get drafted to the Oriole, and rightly so. I mean here I was getting sea time on a ship that never went very far and usually only on weekends, which meant I'd have plenty of time at home with my new family.

We had our own little jetty amongst the auxiliary fleet, a collection of ferries, tugboats and other small watercraft operated and maintained by civilian personnel. We were well away from all the naval pomp and polish, yet there we sat right in the middle of it. Captain Joe's Navy, we used to call it, after the only officer we had onboard, a Lieutenant Commander and Newfoundlander who'd married a wealthy Englishwoman and drove a new 300 SL Mercedes-Benz convertible. If nothing else, Captain Joe was a really flamboyant guy.

The rest of the crew was made up of a Chief Boson by the name of Nick Lazoric, a big man with a thick neck who could charm the birds right out of a tree. Del Hettinger was a Petty Officer 1st class Shipwright, a large man a little overweight with a wonderful personality and sense of humour. Petty Officer 2nd Class Bob McFarland was another great guy. The rest of the crew was made up of three Leading Seamen Bosons and two of us Leading Seamen Stokers, a very top-heavy crew if ever there was one. A lot of chiefs and not nearly enough Indians, in other words.

Captain Joe's armada was made up of the Oriole, a floating workshop (game room as we called it), and the YFP 320. The YFP (Yard Ferry Personnel) was a 40-foot ferry that would normally have carried people back and forth across the harbour, from dockyard to Naden, but this old skiff had been converted. For instance, three high bunks and some lockers had been installed in the aft passenger space, while the forward end belonged to Bob

McFarland and me. They put in bunks, a refrigerator, a small stove and a washroom for the two of us, while the twenty cadets had to share one washroom between them.

McFarland and I were the crew on the YFP; he was the skipper while I was the first mate, engineer, deckhand, cook and everything else. The engine room, located amidships between the two passenger compartments, contained two 250–horsepower Cummins diesels, an electrical diesel generator, and a small boiler for heating the boat and hot water. This was my domain. My reason for being. Besides making coffee, that is.

Once a month we'd take the cadets out on a weekend training cruise, and at night, when we weren't steaming, we'd tie up alongside and the cadets would come aboard to sleep. Otherwise they'd be on the Oriole, learning to sail her.

If you think this sounds a lot like a yacht club, you're right: it was a yacht club. Sometimes, when Captain Joe got the urge, we'd sail up island, or maybe over to Vancouver, Seattle or Port Angeles, which was always nice in the summer. On more than a few of these excursions we wouldn't have the cadets along, and we'd just take the Oriole. After all, Captain Joe might just want to visit a girlfriend or have a party, and the Oriole was much more conducive to such activities.

One thing Captain Joe really enjoyed doing was what was called a "Diesel Stay Sail." For instance, on one occasion, the Oriole sailed proudly into the harbour of Bremerton, Washington which was about two miles wide and five or six miles long, a really big harbour. And when we made the turn to enter and ran into a headwind, Captain Joe would order, "Square tacks and the diesel staysail!" and push forward hard on the throttles.

In these and other such situations, Bob and I, over on the old 320, liked to isolate ourselves from the Oriole and her eccentric Captain Joe. It's not hard to see why. Captain Joe would sail directly across the harbour with the wind abaft the beam and with every working sail full. The Oriole would be heeling over with her lea side gunnels in the water and a big wake boiling up behind her, the 150–horsepower Cummins engine that supplied auxiliary power belching a trail of thick black smoke behind her.

Then, if this weren't bad enough, he'd tack into the wind. The Oriole's sails would languish and start flapping in the breeze until he'd made enough headway to get her a little closer to her finale destination. Then Captain Joe would turn her into another square tack and sail majestically back across the harbour.

There he'd be, Captain Joe, standing proudly at the helm. And next to him would be Nick Lazoric, red-faced and trying to make himself as inconspicuous as possible. If there happened to be cadets onboard, the crew would hide amongst them. And when we didn't have cadets, or the 320, Bob and I would be there, but hiding in the engine room.

One extremely important job, absolutely crucial to national security, with which the Oriole and the YFP were tasked each and every year, occurred during salmon fishing season. The mission was to take the YFP up to Port Alberni, tie up to a log boom, launch a half dozen 12–foot boats with outboard motors, and wait. Then, on the following weekend, ten or twelve high ranking officers, including the Flag Officer of the Pacific Fleet, would come up and fish.

On weekends, Bob and I would make sure the boats were fuelled up at night, and the rest of the crew would clean them as well as any fish our guests happened to catch, packing them on ice. During the week we'd do our regular work. Sometimes, some of the crew would venture out across the log boom and go ashore. In my younger days, I had worked a summer on the log booms at Aleza Lake, so I had enough sense to take my shoes off before venturing out onto the logs. But with a belly full of beer it was still tricky, and I'd inevitably get my feet wet. On more than one occasion, one of the crew who wasn't as fleet of foot or as experienced in alcohol would end up in the drink.

Every year the Oriole was entered in the Swiftsure Sailboat race, from just off the Victoria breakwater out around Swiftsure Rock to the light ship at the entrance to the Strait of Juan de Fuca, a total of 137 miles. This was a tough race—you could run into wind and weather changes the entire distance—and naturally the year I was involved was almost a total disaster. When we finally got out to the start line, she ended up with only enough air to fill her sails, and she wasn't a good sailor in light air. With her nickel-steel hull and wooden masts and spars, she was a heavy boat, and to top it off, just after she was built, she kept breaking the top of her main mast so they shortened it, throwing her out of balance. No, the Oriole was not a good sailor in light air, but give her a good wind and a heavy sea and she could sail with the best of them. She was a tiger out there.

A sailboat is balanced by taking the center of thrust of the combined sails and lining it up with the center of gravity of the hull. Consequently, the old Oriole was a bad boat in light air, and when the gun was fired to start the race, with the tide running against us, we had to drop anchor to keep from going backwards.

We sat up on deck with our sails drawing only enough wind to keep from luffing, watching some of the larger, more modern boats just barely making way. The Diamond Head, out of Hawaii, was one such craft, a real ocean racer able to make way were someone to so much as pass gas in her vicinity. We lined her up with a reference point across the Strait, and then looked away. Then, after a while, we looked back to see how much she had gained—it was never much, but at least she wasn't dragging her anchor.

After an hour or two, a little squall blew in and we were finally on our way, but by this time everyone else was moving well ahead of us. The wind blew down the Strait, forcing us to tack against it. We weren't making very good time, but at least we were moving, getting out of the overly critical scrutiny of the many spectators lining the shore.

We fought a headwind the rest of the day, but it was freshening and by the time we rounded the light ship and Race Rocks we had a good wind on our stern. When sailing into the wind, you sail as close to it as possible. This means you're always working, adjusting the sails continuously, and it is hard work, no two ways about it. Running with the wind is always more relaxing.

Although we were too far behind to catch the other larger boats, it was exhilarating to be sailing. To be *really* sailing. We were almost running in a gale force wind that night; we could feel the vibration of the freewheeling propeller as it started turning a speed never attained while under power.

Early the following morning, as we sailed towards Victoria, Captain Joe had every inch of the Oriole's 6133 square foot of working sail drawing wind, even though, with this kind of wind, they should have been shortened. And as we rounded the corner heading toward Victoria Harbour, in an act of defiance to the gods of the sea, he called out an order that shocked everyone.

"Make ready the spinnaker," he said.

To a man, we looked at him aghast.

"Make ready the spinnaker," he repeated, and the crew did as asked. Then he said, "Hoist the spinnaker." Now this was an evolution the crew had practiced and performed many times, but never in this kind of weather. We had to fight to get the furled spinnaker rigged and up into place.

Everyone waited for Captain Joe to give the order. There seemed to be a hesitation. Was Captain Joe having second thoughts? Not on your life. Not our flamboyant Captain Joe. "Unfurl the spinnaker," he said, and we pulled the lashings. There was another hesitation, as if the Oriole herself were somehow reluctant to employ more sail, and then with a crack the spinnaker opened and took wind.

The crew held their collective breath. No one on deck dared take their eyes from the mast and rigging, expecting everything to come crashing down around them at any moment. The Oriole jumped forward as she took the bone in her teeth, but everything seemed to be holding together. What a fine old boat, we were thinking. I mean here she was, over half a century old, and doing something no one would even consider doing with a new boat.

Standing at the wheel with a look that said, "Yes, I am indeed the man," Captain Joe was looking out upon his crew all smiles and pats on the back when there occurred a loud "boom" that sounded just like a cannon shot. Every man's head snapped aloft to see our spinnaker in shreds, the tattered remains of 7000 square feet of light nylon flapping in the wind. The old boat had taken it, but the pressure had proven too much for the more modern nylon. Unfortunately though, only Captain Joe and his loyal crew witnessed the miraculous event, alone in the darkness of early morning as we sailed unceremoniously and with no audience, no applause, and dead last into Victoria Harbour.

I can imagine the sight the old girl would have provided for anyone onshore, had there been anyone onshore to see it. The Oriole, with her bow down from all the sail she was carrying at better than 16 knots, knifing her way through sea, spray flying over the deck. In my mind I can see her even now, a very old lady in a white gown, lifting her skirts as she runs across a dark watery field in the rain.

The beauty of being engineer on the YFP was that she was part of the Auxiliary Fleet and not really part of the navy. I didn't perform any maintenance on her machinery; the civilian dock-yard maties did all that. I would simply make out a work order and they would come and do it, no questions asked. During the summer I spent many hours painting on the upper deck, and in the winter I found plenty of things to occupy my time below. All in all, I did pretty well what I wanted to, and it was a good life. Bob Macfarlane was my boss, but he was a laid back kind of guy and we had a good working relationship.

When we were at sea with cadets they would all be onboard the Oriole during the day, so Bob and I would have the YFP to ourselves. Bob would sit on his stool at the helm, running the boat, while I would piddle around, or else sit on the settee behind him and read or shoot the breeze.

One sunny summer Friday morning, with Captain Joe off on a date or something, the Oriole was taking long tacks with the diesel staysail hammering away, creating a very large wake. Bob was at the helm of the YFP and I was lounging leisurely on the settee behind him. He had a chart of the waters we were steam-ing in, and I noticed he was studying it pretty intently. Eventually he handed me the binoculars and said, "Hey Mel, do you see that rock and marker buoy up ahead there, just to port?"

I took the binoculars and had a look. "I see them, but aren't they steaming far enough to starboard to miss them?" I asked.

"Well, look here on the chart. See how this rock drops off to starboard and then levels off? It tells you right here: this part of the rock isn't visible at high tide, and this is high tide. I wonder if they have a cadet navigating out there."

As we watched the Oriole close in on the rock, Bob said, "Although we don't draw as much water as they do, I'm going to move a little to starboard just to be safe."

A few painful seconds passed as we sat there waiting impatiently for the Oriole to change course. "Aren't you going to radio them and tell them about it?" I eventually asked.

Bob though for a while, then finally said, "No, I don't think so. They're supposed to be the smart ones, they'll find out soon enough."

We sat there watching the Oriole through our glasses. We were just about alongside now, but we thought we should keep a good eye out in case someone went overboard. Then all at once the stern rose out of the water, the mast racked forward, and she bounced across the shoal before finally levelling out.

"Yup, I told you they were too close," Bob said as he folded up his chart and put it away with a laugh.

17

I sailed on the Oriole until August 31, 1960, just twenty-four days short of a year, at which point I was drafted back to Naden for a Trade Group Two Engineering Course. It was a little disappointing to leave her, but I needed the course to get promoted, so to the delight of my family I would be living back ashore.

We were late getting back into harbour the day I was supposed to start my course, so by the time I got to Naden and did my in-routine it was too late to join my class. I went the next morning instead after obtaining my schedule from the office in the engineering school, a very large building on the base complete with schoolrooms and workshops of all kinds, including machine shops, steam engineering shops and a diesel shop.

According to my schedule I was supposed to be in a math class, and after wandering around a while I eventually found the right room. I knocked on the door and walked in. A roomful of hands confronted me, none of whom I recognized.

"I can only assume you must be the late Leading Seaman McConaghy?" the lieutenant at the front of the room asked, and everyone laughed.

"Yes, sir," I answered in what I thought was an indignant tone of voice. This guy looked to be all of twenty-five years old.

"I'm Lieutenant Smart. Grab yourself a desk, McConaghy. You haven't missed that much," he said, and went right back to the lesson he was teaching.

As I found myself a desk, I glanced around for a familiar face amongst the fifteen other Leading Seamen seated in the room. I didn't recognize anyone, nor was there any sign that anyone recognized me. This was understandable though, considering the fact I'd been away from General Service for almost two years.

One person I do remember from the first day is Dave McCallum. Dave was a big man, about 6–foot, maybe a little taller, and weighed around 200 pounds. He was a handsome guy with dark straight hair, but the reason I remember him specifically has nothing to do with his good looks. I soon caught wind that his wife had given birth just a couple of days previous and, as was the tradition, he'd been out celebrating the night before. He had a tremendous hangover and everyone in the class, including Lieutenant Smart, was giving him a good-natured bad time. Dave and I ended up sailing together on our next ship along with a number of guys from the class.

But that first day I had yet to meet anyone, and Lieutenant Smart continued on with the lesson as though I'd been there all along. I couldn't help but notice his enthusiasm for the subject matter, and the fact that, although he'd only met the class the day before, he seemed to know all their names. This man, I would soon realize, was one of the finest teachers I'd ever meet. When teaching, he would get so excited about his subject he would actually bounce up and down. It was simply impossible for his students not to share in his enthusiasm and learn the material.

But there at the beginning I was not so sure. Lieutenant Smart was supposed to be teaching us an equivalent of grade twelve math, algebra and something called Pythagoras Theorem. "Pythagoras Theorem," I thought. "What the hell is Pythagoras Theorem?" I sat at my desk dumfounded, glancing every so often at the door, thinking very seriously about abandoning the whole notion of career advancement. This guy wouldn't have a chance in hell of teaching me anything, let alone this mystical and menacing Pythagoras Theorem.

I stayed though, and eventually started to get to know the rest of the class. Some, like me, were high school dropouts, while others had achieved varying degrees of education right up to and including grade twelve. The latter didn't have near the difficulty with this stuff that I had. For instance, one day Lt. Smart was trying to teach us algebra. On the blackboard he made a certain triangle with the letters A, B and C at the corners. Then he gave the letters A and B values and asked the class what the value of C would be. The ensuing silence was deafening, so he decided to solve it for us. Then he turned around and faced the class, only to find a fellow by the name of Doug Hudson sitting by the window, leaning on his elbow, dreamily watching the birds flit through the trees outside.

Lt. Smart looked at him and said, "Mr. Hudson, I suppose you can solve this problem?"

"Yes, sir. But I wouldn't do it the way you did."

"Well then, Mr. Hudson, will you kindly come up here to the blackboard and show us exactly how you would solve it?"

Doug got up with a bored look on his face and proceeded to show Lt. Smart exactly how he would have solved the problem.

"Thank you, Mr. Hudson, you can sit down now and watch the birds. I'll wake you up when the course is over, with an A I would imagine."

There were plenty of us on the course that didn't have the education of Doug Hudson, and when we ran into a problem I think Lt. Smart relished the opportunity to educate us. He didn't look down on us, but used his skill and enthusiasm to drill the lesson into our thick heads. I cannot think of enough words of praise for this man.

The Trade Group Two Engineering Course consisted not only of Lt. Smart's academics classes, but of engineering theory and practical experience as well. We spent many a day tearing apart different pieces of machinery like diesel engines and putting them back together again. We made toolboxes in the sheet metal shop and all sorts of goodies in the machine shop to put in our toolboxes, which we then took home so that at some point, when our wives got tired of moving them around, they could throw them away.

After four months of Lt. Smart jumping around and aging at least three years, we all passed the course. I didn't get a ship right away, so I hung around Naden for the next eight months as the Corporal of the Gangway, a special duty job that mostly entailed sitting at the main gate for eight hours making sure anyone going ashore or coming aboard was in fact permitted to do so. This was almost a civilian job and the family loved it. We were situated in an office with a commissionaire, usually a retired serviceman, and when anyone below a commissioned officer went ashore we'd take their Station Card, which told us what part of the watch they were on, giving it back to them upon their return.

I think at this point I should explain what a Station Card is. It's a little book, not unlike a passport, that if you were on the Starboard watch was green and if you were on the Port watch was red. It was issued to you when you joined a new ship or station and was a very efficient means of keeping track of your where-abouts. If you didn't have it, you were trapped onboard. The two pages inside contained your name, rank, serial number and where you were employed. If you were asked for it and couldn't produce it you were in trouble, almost like getting caught for speeding and not being able to produce your driver's license. The underage hands had a "UA" stamped across their cards, which were placed in their own special rack. At the witching hour of midnight you would pull these cards, and when the Duty Officer made his rounds of the base you'd hand them over, and the offending hand would be "in the shit," as it was commonly called.

One of the Commissionaires I used to stand watch with was an old retired army fellow whose name escapes me now. He was seventy years old, a widower, and had a terrific sense of humour. One night, when we were on the midnight to 0800 watch, he told me he'd started taking Geritol.

"Did it do you any good?"

"Yeah, sure it did. But I had to give it up."

"If it was working for you, why would you give it up?" I asked.

"Well as you know, I'm a widower and I live alone. I started having wet dreams and I sure as hell can't afford hookers."

We both laughed.

That was a good year I spent ashore, but as was the nature of the trade they never left us stokers ashore too long. Eventually I was once again drafted back to sea, much to the dismay of my wife and growing family.

18

I reported to the HMCS Stettler on April 28, 1961, happy to be back aboard another Prestonian Class Frigate. When I joined her she was just finishing a refit in dry dock. I was surprised to find out three of the hands that had been on the course with me the year before were joining her as well: Dave McCallum, Gordy Rieser and Ross Haynes. The first job I was assigned to was in the engine room, and this suited me just fine. As I have said before, these engines were poetry in motion.

Being the senior Leading Seaman Stoker onboard, I was in charge of everyone working in the engine room and in our mess deck from Leading Seaman on down. I would assign the A/B and O/D stokers the jobs assisting the P/1s and P/2s assigned to the senior P/1 of the engine room by the Chief Petty Officer, First Class Engine Room Artificer, or to make it slightly more ambiguous, the C/1ERA, who in turn was responsible to the Engineering Officer, who was responsible to the Captain. The person issuing the order, at each particular level, wrote out each order, or at least that's the way it was suppose to work.

Normally what happened was the C/1ERA would give the Senior Hand of each machinery space a list of things that needed to be done, while he himself sat around the breakfast table having coffee. Then P/1ERA Jim Spencer would shout down to me in the engine room as he came down the ladder:

"McConaghy, I need three good hands to help on (insert whatever job needed to be done), and take the rest of the hands and get those fucking bilges cleaned up." And so goes the chain of command.

Jim Spencer was an Englishman who'd been tossed from his own country or perhaps immigrated to Canada of his own accord and somehow ended up in the Canadian Navy. There was almost always a little friction between us that was never really serious and after I was drafted disappeared almost entirely, but while we worked together was always there.

He would say things like, "McConaghy, just because you sailed with the Queen, that don't cut no ice here."

"Listen, you British Empire DP, neither does your accent," I'd shoot back, or else something like: "If you learned to talk right, maybe we could understand you." It was a little bit of one-upmanship, I think, but it was usually restricted to the engine room.

Our Skipper was a Senior Lieutenant Commander by the name of Vondette, or "Old Guns" as the crew affectionately referred to him. He'd been a Gunnery Officer in the old navy before they unified and made all officers general list. In the new navy no officer had a specialized trade: on one ship he could be the Supply Officer and on another he could be the Engineering Officer. The decisions pertaining to a particular department were left to the Senior Chief Petty Officers of that department, but in the officers' defence, they all had to know how to handle a ship and navigate.

Old Guns loved to shoot, and he was good at it. When we went out on a gunnery shoot, a marksmanship competition between ships, it didn't matter whom we were shooting against as we would always win. We could be shooting against other frigates, or our new destroyer escorts with their new rapid-firing, radar-controlled 3.5–inch guns, or the Yanks with their own rapidly expanding arsenal, and we would always outshoot them. Old Guns had a few secret weapons, most notably his gun crews.

We had a mounting of two 4–inch guns located forward of the bridge, and part of its gun crew was a man by the name of Ferguson. Ferguson wasn't all that good a sailor—he liked to drink, maybe a little too much, didn't worry too much about getting back to the ship on time, and could be depended on to be adrift at least once a month. He could be best described as a bad ass, but he had one enduring quality that appealed to the old man: Ferguson could shoot those big guns.

The ship and its guns were vintage World War II, so each gun crew consisted of a Layer, who controlled the horizontal movement of the guns, and a Trainer, who controlled the vertical movement of the gun and the trigger. Ferguson was the Trainer.

On the bridge, the Gunnery Officer would identify the target, relaying the bearing and range over the intercom. The bearing wasn't too much of a problem; the Layer simply swung the gun and pointed it at the target. While he was doing this, the Trainer would elevate the guns to the predetermined elevation so that the projectile would travel the predetermined arc to achieve the right range, and when they were on-target and the Gunnery Officer shouted, "Shoot!" the Trainer would pull the trigger, the guns would go boom, and the projectile would hopefully hit the target. Simple, right?

Not really. We were at sea here, remember, and there was a very good possibility the ship would be rolling. The Layer just had to keep his crosshairs on the target. The Trainer, on the other hand, would have to compensate for the roll of the ship. If the guns went down the shot would be short, and if the guns went up the shot would be long, in either case missing the target. Ferguson, though, was a genius at pulling the trigger at just the right time, and the old man loved him for it.

We also had another gunner onboard, a native Canadian by the name of Charley Rabbit. Charley came from the badlands of southern Alberta and learned how to hunt at an early age. On the starboard side of the bridge was a mounting consisting of one 40mm anti-aircraft Bofor. There were a few more Bofors located throughout the ship, but this one was Charlie's gun.

One time we were doing an anti-aircraft shoot just after tot time. Of course Charley was at his trusty gun, and on a single Bofor like Charlie's, one person controlled every operation except loading. The exercise consisted of an aircraft pulling a drone behind it on a long cable, reminiscent of a windsock you see at airports.

The Gunnery Officer called out the order for Charley to shoot. Charley opened fire, and after a few rounds hit the cable on the drone and it came fluttering down. But Charley kept shooting, steadily walking his rounds towards the tow plane. The Gunnery Officer shouted over the intercom, "Check firing!" but still Charley kept his finger on the trigger. The Gunnery Officer began to panic. "Check! Check! Check!" he yelled until Charlie's loader stopped loading the gun and he ran out of ammo.

Afterwards it came to light that Charley had partaken of a couple of tots before lunch, and as a result had found himself back in the badlands, shooting rabbits. Later, I was told by one of the lookouts on the bridge that day, that when the Gunnery Officer was ranting on the bridge afterwards about how old Charley was going to be when he finally got out of the brig, the old man turned to him and said, "Good shooting, though, don't you think?"

"Yes, sir," said the Gunnery Officer. And that was the end of it.

On the Stettler we were doing pretty much as we'd done on the other frigates, the "Triangle Run" as it was called, training officer cadets. The only things that changed were the ports of call. We always started in Esquimalt, but then went somewhere in California before heading over to the Hawaiian Islands and back to Esquimalt, or else the reverse. And we would usually take a little trip down to Seattle or some other port in Washington or Oregon so we could march in the 4th of July parade too. Every once in a while we'd do a Queen Charlotte patrol in search of Russian subs, and when that got tiring we'd chase the Grilse, our own beleaguered submarine, around the Pacific Ocean. I've personally known men who spent their entire naval careers doing just that. I guess I was very fortunate in the fact that although I saw a lot of ships in my ten-year career, I saw a lot of variety too.

On a Triangle Run there was a ritual we never failed to engage in, especially in Hawaii. There has been a great deal of debate as to when and where this ritual was born, and no one can say for sure, though it had been occurring since before I joined the navy, that much is certain. Every time we tied up in Pearl Harbor, we'd be assigned a host ship from the "semi" fleet. Semi was the term we used for the American navy, because all over their ships were plastered little signs that said semi-automatic this and semi-automatic that. Anyway, it never failed that we'd be challenged to a game of beer ball by our semi, although it was never called beer ball on the official invitation. But we could read between the lines. Then, on the appointed day, we'd fill a big cooler with a few dozen beer, pack the beer with ice, and just to make it look good, throw a top layer of pop in. In retrospect I don't know who we thought we were fooling; everybody knew what was going on.

Finally a bus would pull up to the jetty and we'd load up, filling the bus with our players, our officials, our fans, and of course our cooler. When we eventually got to the field, everyone would unload as one laughing reeling mob, much to the delight of our opponents. As often as not we'd be greeted by two or three washtubs full of American beer on ice, with the requisite amount of pop on top as acting camouflage.

Maybe I should explain the rules of the game of beer ball. By and large they were the same as regular softball, but with a few key modifications. The scorecard had only two or three innings, and a base runner had to stop at every base and chug a beer before continuing on to the next base. As you've probably figured out, this was why there were only two or three innings on the scorecard. I never remember a game going any longer than that, but that being said they could last almost as long as a cricket match.

Along with his standard duties, the scorekeeper was also in charge of the beer runners, which meant he had to run a full beer out to whatever base the runner was on after he'd emptied his previous one. The scorekeeper had easy access to the beer and was usually the first man to falter, never making it past three innings.

One game at the naval air station at Barbers Point, across the harbour from Pearl, Ross Haines twisted his knee. At the time it was thought he might have broken a bone or torn a ligament or worse, possibly something much worse, because in all honesty the man was whining like a baby. As punishment for sporting such a low pain threshold, we left him out there in the field to bake in the sun until halfway through the second inning when, too drunk to continue, we finished the game. The buses hadn't come yet, so we were all lying around under the palm trees drinking the last of the beer, all of us except Ross, who was still out there alone. To add insult to injury, there was now only American beer remaining, as the Yanks liked ours more than their own.

By this time Ross's knee was swollen, and whenever he was whining a little too much someone would walk over to where he was lying and give it a little tap and accuse him of being a baby. Now you might think this was a little cruel, but at the time we thought it was great fun and besides, we didn't want the Yanks to think we were a bunch of softies. Saving face was an integral part of beer ball.

But it wasn't all fun and games on the Stettler. After a couple of months I was made Upper Deck Stoker, my new job consisting mainly of watching over all the fuel and fresh water onboard, the stability of the ship, and the machinery on the upper deck including the diesel engine on the motor cutter. The Upper Deck Stoker was a special duty job, meaning I didn't stand watch at sea or in harbour.

A typical day would see me get up at 0500, shower, shave and get a coffee which, if the weather was nice, I would drink up top on the quarterdeck. Otherwise I would drink it in the cafeteria with some of the other hands. At this time of the morning, before the wakeup call, some of the older hands who wanted to miss the rush in the washroom were up having their morning coffee as well.

The first thing I would do was sound the fuel tanks. Located on the inboard side of the hull and following its contours, their size depended on what needed to be placed beside or above them. They were connected by main suction lines and isolated by valves, and you always used two tanks directly across from each other so that the ship maintained an even keel.

To sound the tanks, you unscrewed the fitting at the top of the sounding tube that was always flush with the deck in whatever compartment it happened to be in. Then you dropped the weighted end of a twenty-foot tape measure into the sounding tube until it almost touched the bottom of the tank. Then you waited until the ship was as close to level as possible, at which point you dropped the tape measure to the bottom. Now you had a reading, which you checked against the brass plaque on the bulkhead next to the sounding tube that gave the capacity of the tank and how much fuel it contained.

Next you sounded the freshwater tanks. The procedure was the same (though of course the tape measure was different), and once you had all your readings you wrote out your report and presented it to Engineering Officer, who in turn presented it to the Captain. This procedure was performed at 0800 and at 2000 every day, without exception. This little evolution might seem like a minor one, but such information was crucial to a warship. For obvious reasons, the captain needed to know exactly how much fuel was onboard at all times, and in the case of an emergency, how far the ship could steam, at what speed, and how much fuel it would need to take on when it reached its next port or refuelling tanker were all of paramount importance. Running out of fuel at sea was simply not an option. Running out of fuel meant death to a warship.

When you were steaming in a high sea and the ship was rolling heavily and ploughing into wave after wave, almost bringing it to a shuddering stop, sounding the tanks became a nearly impossible task, but even when the fuel was sloshing around in the tank in a light swell it could prove tricky. I found that in such situations, knowing just how deep the tank was, and holding the tape at the precise depth of the tank, if you hung a weighted string in a spot where you could line it up with two vertical bulkheads, one running abaft the beam and one fore and aft, at the moment the string lined up with the bulkheads you could very quickly sound the tank. Considering the depth and length of each pair of tanks was different, it was a complicated process.

During the day, knowing how much fuel was in the tanks you were steaming on, you could change them over before running them dry. At night you would note in the engine room orders for the tanks to be changed over at a certain time. Most of the bigger tanks were located on either side of the boiler and engine rooms because they were the easiest to fill when you were refuelling, even if the sounding tube always seemed to be in a tiled deck space.

Refuelling was another responsibility of the Upper Deck Stoker and was performed as soon as the ship was secured to the dock. You would be informed well before you tied up just how big the line from shore was and what type of connections you'd need so that everything would be ready when the time arrived. Once the ship was hooked up to the refuelling station, they would immediately start pumping, so it was a good idea to have a hand ready at each of the tank's sounding tubes and corresponding valves. The first part of the evolution was fairly easy, but as the tanks started to top off things could get a little hectic and everyone had to be on their toes. As the tanks filled and you started shutting them down one after another, the flow increased to the next open tank.

Most of the American bases were fitted with 8– to 10–inch refuelling hoses, while we had 6–inch pipes onboard. Even at reduced pressure the flow would steadily increase, and if you didn't get a valve closed in time you'd have yourself one hell of a spill. I can tell you from firsthand experience that Bunker B fuel oil is not the type of thing you want to be cleaning up in a galley or any other place.

The Upper Deck Stoker was also responsible for the capstan on the foc'sil, the motor cutter, and every other piece of equipment not actually located in a machinery space that didn't require a watch-keeper. All in all it was a good job, and I quite enjoyed my time in the position, but eventually I left the Stettler for a month to take a Clearance Diver course anyway.

Most ships weren't large enough to carry a team of regular divers, so they trained existing hands who qualified. Of course I qualified, even though I couldn't swim very well and hadn't so much as passed the swimming test in basic training. However, not to be deterred, I managed to convince the Personnel Selection Officer that it must have been an administrational mistake. After all, how could a guy from a place called Aleza Lake be unable to swim for Christ's sake? Moreover, it was my personal theory that being a good swimmer didn't necessarily correlate to being a good diver, because having spent all one's time trying to stay on top of the water might actually prove a hindrance in learning to live under it.

We were still at sea when the course started, so again, as was seemingly the custom, I managed to miss the first two days. Nothing important, mind you, just the classes in which, in a nice heated swimming pool in Naden, they taught the rest of the class how to put on a diving suit and how to use the breathing apparatus.

I arrived at the diving unit just in time to be issued my equipment and told that after supper that night, at 1700 hours, I'd be making a night dive. At that time wetsuits were primarily being used, but only qualified divers got them. The suits we newbies were given were like condoms, Bell-Aquas and Dunlops. They were called drysuits, and you wore Angora long johns under them or else you froze to death.

The Bell-Aqua was a light rubber suit with a hole right in the middle of the stomach you stepped into, pulled up to your waist, and then pulled up over your arms, upper body and head. Then you took the excess from around the waist and rolled it up and tied it with a piece of surgical rubber tubing. All very precise to be sure.

Myself, though, I got a Dunlop suit, and when I first saw it, it looked like it could stand up by itself. My first thought was that it must have been made of old truck tire tubes. I studied it thoroughly, and the only place I could find to get into it was through the neck, a hole about ten inches in diameter surrounded by a heavier rubber than the rest of the suit. There was also a hood with what looked like a hose clamp attached, the same size as the hole at the top of the suit. This made sense somewhat.

That night, at exactly 1630, I submitted myself to the torture of getting into this throwback from the First World War. First I put one foot through the hole in the neck and then, with the help of my partner pulling on one side of it and stretching it open, I got the other foot in. Then, with a lot of stretching, pulling and grunting, we got the suit up around my waist, cutting off the circulation to the lower half of my body and cranking my long johns up around my crotch so tight my voice went up at least four octaves. The thought immediately crossed my mind: "My God, my wife goes through this everyday, getting into her girdle." If nothing else, that course instilled in me a newfound respect for womankind.

Unfortunately, what I had just accomplished was the easy part. Next my buddy stretched the neck so that I could get my right arm into the sleeve. Then he went around and stretched the other side so that I could get my left arm and the rest of my body in. This proved excruciatingly difficult, but finally we did it and sat down and rested. The remainder was much easier: I put the big hose clamp over my head and pulled the hood over it, then sealed the hood to the neck. Still, I was exhausted. I remember sitting there thinking, "I'm going to have to do this twice a day, five day a week, for the next *month*? I think I'll quit." But of course I didn't.

That night is permanently etched in my mind. Once dressed, we were double-marched down to the tank storage building where we were issued our air tanks for the dive. Then we were double-marched down to the wharf where we'd be diving, and where we finished suiting up. I would like to remind you that to this point in my life I had never so much as had a mouthpiece in my mouth, let alone tried to breathe through one. I had no idea whatsoever what was going on, but still I soldiered on.

They lined six of us up, each with a shot line in front of us (a shot line being a big piece of rope with a heavy weight tied to the end to keep it taut), then someone shouted, "Everyone in the water!" I was petrified, and stood there like a statue, an effigy to reluctant divers the world over. And then someone else pushed me in.

I gagged on my mouthpiece, trying to breathe through my nose. The cold water was seeping through cracks in the backs of my knees, crotch and armpits, slashing my skin like cold knives. I found the shot line and grabbed hold of it with a death grip, about to start for the surface. My face mask was tight up against the shot line which, when I finally opened my eyes, was the only thing I could see except for my hands and the bubbles I was making. I was at this moment as close to having a heart attack as I've ever been in my seven-plus decades of life. Suddenly something grabbed my shoulder and I spun around ready to fight whatever monster of the deep might be looking to have me for supper.

Seeing I was having trouble, Ernie Maddens, one of the standby divers, took me by the arms and held the palm of his hand in front of my face to indicate that everything was okay. Then, pointing in the direction of the sea bottom twenty feet below, he took me by the hand and slowly swam me down.

When I finally started to get my breath and relaxed, it was actually quite an amazing experience. A feeling of calm came over me, and except for the icy cold Pacific Ocean slowly seeping into my suit, I really started to enjoy the dive. And soon even the water in my suit began to warm up from my body heat. From that point on I never looked back, but I can tell you this, if it hadn't been for Ernie Maddens and his timely hand on my shoulder, I would have quit right there on the spot.

I returned to my ship a qualified Clearance Diver. Soon thereafter I was issued my wetsuit, and I could get into it by myself with very little effort. At the time we were getting 6 cents a minute while we were diving, or $3.60 an hour, but when you were only taking home $360 a month it all helped.

We did training dives when we were in harbour, at home and on duty. Usually after 1600 we'd go down, chase crabs and bring them back to the galley, as the cooks were more than happy to cook them up for a share.

On one trip to Pearl Harbor I'd been ashore after a ball game, and returned to the ship around 0100. We were sailing that morning, and I didn't have much to do except man the capstan while leaving harbour, one of my jobs as Upper Deck Stoker. The capstan was the winch that raised the anchor, and it was run by a small steam engine.

Around 0530, a big stoker by the name of Garnet King woke me up. He was on the flash-up watch that morning (the flash-up being when they fired up the boilers and readied the machinery spaces for sea), and the engine room watch had gone back to the steering compartment to start the steering engine and to grease the bearing on the A bracket. This A bracket was an inverted A-shaped bracket that supported the propellers and propeller shafts at the stern of the ship, and they were greased by turning a hand wheel connected to a threaded spindle that forced grease down to a teak bearing inside. It was greased once every watch by the engine room stoker, and before the ship went to sea.

On this particular morning one of the brackets wasn't taking grease, so as resident Clearance Divers it fell to Garnet and me to find out why. We'd need to take a crescent wrench to the offending bracket's corresponding threaded plug while they were turning the hand wheel on the surface. This was an engineering problem, and being the senior man in that department I was required to make the dive.

It was still dark out, so I insisted on a safety line, an eight-foot rope we tied to our wrists. Well I was still adjusting my facemask when big Garnet went over the side taking me with him, head first. When I finally got straightened out, and finished straightening him out, we swam down and pulled the plug. Garnet handed it to me and tapped on the hull, signalling the hand to turn the wheel on the greaser. Immediately air began bubbling out of the hole, indicating an air lock. When it eventually cleared, Garnet tapped on the hull signalling the hand to stop turning the wheel. And that's when I dropped the plug. I looked at Garnet, Garnet looked at me, and then we shrugged and swam down to the bottom to look for it, but with all the silt it proved impossible to find. So we swam to the surface to get another one.

"We need another plug," Garnet shouted up to the deck once we reached the surface.

"What happened to the other one?" someone on deck shouted down.

"Oh, McConaghy here fumbled it. Must've thought he was still playing ball."

They took off to the workshop to get another plug, and when they finally got back and lowered it on a line, it had a big hoop welded to it.

"There. Put it around his neck and maybe he'll be able to hang onto it."

Now I didn't make a lot of mistakes on the job, but about this time I was starting to notice I was being passed over for promotion. This was at the time when the federal government was unifying the services, and they'd changed the enlistment time to three years instead of five. Sometime earlier I'd applied for submarine service, and in late August I was finally drafted to the HMCS Grilse, our one and only submarine on the West Coast.

19

The Grilse was an old WWII fleet class boat borrowed from the Americans, and unlike some of the boats the Canadian Navy has received from their British counterparts of late, it was a good one. Not surprisingly, life on a submarine was completely different than on any other ship in the navy. It was like living in a sewer pipe, and submariners deserved every extra penny they were paid and then some.

The bunk I was assigned to was a top bunk, and when I climbed into it, if I wanted to turn over, I'd have to slide out of it and roll over and then slide back in. We each had a tiny little locker where we kept one extra pair of work clothes, our shaving kit and a couple of extra changes of underwear, while everyone hung their uniforms in the same place.

There was one little sink in the aft torpedo room for about thirty men, and while there were three showers onboard, we weren't allowed to use them because we were always short of water. When our dungarees or whatever we wore at sea got dirty, we simply folded them and put them between the mattress and springs of our bunks. And when it was time to change and we'd worn all our clean outfits, we'd take these ones out all nicely pressed and ready to go, and rotate them in. The clothing worn at sea was optional, and some of the outfits the hands wore were anything but navy issue.

There were four toilets onboard, and when we were at sea, hiding from surface ships and/or aircraft that were trying and failing to find us, we could only use one of the two that discharged into a sanitary tank located inboard of the pressure hull. The others flushed outside the hull through an elaborate series of pipes and valves that if you didn't open and close in the right sequence would blow back in your face. This was not a pleasant experience.

Every night at midnight we would blow the sanitary tanks overboard, which would immediately vent back into the aft battery space located between the cafeteria and the forward engine room. As a result, this space was used primarily to stow the garbage that wasn't thrown overboard while we were on exercises, as doing so would give away our position. More importantly, however, it was where we drank our tots.

From the outside, a submarine is little more than it appears to be: a very large tube able to withstand extremely high pressure. The inside, however, contains various pieces of delicate equipment and a (hopefully) not-so-delicate crew, each compartment of which is accessed via watertight hatches. Around the outside of the pressure hull is the casing, the part you see in pictures, and the fuel and air tanks are located between these two hulls.

Being lighter than water, the fuel was held in the tanks and forced into the pressure hull by water pressure, at which point it was run through a purifying separator before being pumped into a ready-use tank for the engines. It was not uncommon, then, when going to sea, to fill the bilges with diesel fuel to extend the range of the boat, a nice little addition that only added to the unique aroma of a submarine at sea. Needless to say, it was always nice to return to harbour if for no other reason than to open the hatches and get a wholesale change of air. When I returned home from a trip, before I entered the house, my wife would make me change in the entranceway and hang my work clothes outside. Generally speaking, a submariner wasn't a pleasant smelling fellow.

On the surface, the Grilse was propelled by four big diesel engines generating power through each engine's generator, two per engine room, and while submerged, by electric motors powered by batteries that took up almost half the boat. When on watch in the engine room, standing between two 1600 HP engines so that you could reach them both at the same time, the noise was deafening. Shout as loud as you want, you won't hear yourself. The boat could run on one engine on the surface while the remaining three charged batteries, or any other combination.

Once a day the Grilse's enormous batteries had to be recharged, which, while on exercises, was performed in darkness so as to maintain stealth. The big engines used massive quantities of air, so when we were recharging at night it was with the boat floating just under the surface with only a snorkel, a very small radar mast and the periscope above the surface. If the sea was rough and a wave flooded the snorkel head, censors would close it, causing a vacuum in the boat.

To prevent this rapid and extreme change in pressure from blowing out the crew's eardrums and melting down the engines, a device called a flameout valve was installed that would shut down the engines when the air dropped to a predetermined pressure. I've been told that, on more than one occasion while fumigating a similar boat, the Americans melted down an engine. They would clear the boat, tighten down the hatches, leave an engine running and inject pesticide into the boat. When the engine had evacuated all the inside air, the engine would flame out and stop. If the flameout valve didn't work, the engine would run to destruction.

Snorkelling had other uncomfortable side effects, like condensation. When the weather was bad outside and large amounts of cold air were being pulled into a warm boat, you would get a deluge of it. Everything in the boat would be dripping with condensation, but of course you were prepared for this. Mattresses and bedding were encased in a large vinyl bag, with clothes placed underneath. What you couldn't prepare for was waking up with a massive headache from the pressure changes. It was like flying from ground level to 12,000 feet in seconds, every few minutes, and it was nauseating.

The main purpose for having a submarine on the West Coast, especially one as old as the Grilse, was to train the surface ships in anti-submarine warfare. Typically we started charging our batteries on Saturday afternoon. We would start around noon with four engines online, and as the charge came up we would cut off engines one after another until we only had one engine running by early the next morning, levelling out the charge in the batteries. Then, around 1600 Sunday, we would go to sea so we could be "on station" when the squadron that would be searching for us would leave harbour around 0800 Monday morning.

What followed was a game of hide and seek until around noon on Friday when, having failed to find us, the surface ships would leave for home at high speed. They would be in harbour around 1600, while we wouldn't get in until 1900, at which point we'd start charging our batteries again Saturday afternoon.

It was one of these Saturday afternoons that the Skipper came down to have a chat with us. A few of us were sitting in the cafeteria having coffee when he came in and sat down. Not surprisingly the conversation quickly turned, and the Skipper mentioned how lucky we were to have all this security and a steady job.

"You know," he said, "there are people out there with nothing who are starving."

Well this was too much for me.

"You know, sir, there are people out there, friends of mine I went to school with in fact, who are well on their way to becoming millionaires. I think that, in this day and age, anyone who is starving deserves to starve." It wasn't long after this ill-timed outburst that I was drafted off the boat. Apparently, in the eyes of the Skipper, I wasn't mentally fit for submarine service. He was nothing if not a gung-ho navy man.

I left the boat with mixed emotions. I enjoyed the challenges it offered me, and the pride in knowing I was well on my way to becoming a qualified submariner. But I was really pissed off when on my departing assessment I was given a "satisfactory" and not a "superior" for the first time since 1956.

I wasn't too happy to realize that a disagreement with a superior, whose somewhat misguided and narrow-minded views on the country and the world had been formed, at least in part, by a view through a periscope, could spoil my career. But apparently it could.

20

At 441 feet in length, the Cape Breton was classified as an Escort Maintenance vessel and looked more like a freighter than a warship. She had a massive machine shop, a welding shop and a foundry for making steel and iron casting, and her job was to follow any of the anti-submarine squadrons, doing whatever repairs were required.

In reality this never happened. In fact, her real beauty was the fact she hardly ever went to sea. It was like having a shore draft, but with all the shipboard benefits like rum, duty free cigarettes and the possibility that maybe one day you might go to sea. Another benefit was the room. There was lots of it. And at a sedate eleven knots, she waddled along at sea like a big old fat lady, but she was comfortable while she was at it.

The first job I got was steaming and day-working in the engine/boiler room. The space was massive: four decks high and extending the full width of the ship, and the main engine was the granddaddy of all engines. When you walked into this space the first things you saw were the tops of the cylinder heads, and being a triple-expansion engine, the same as they had in the frigates, the low-pressure cylinder head was ten feet across and the entire engine stood three decks high. No exaggeration, you could ride a bicycle around the top of the low-pressure cylinder. The boiler sat just to the stern of the main engine and off to the port side.

After having sailed on a submarine where everything was within arm's reach and the crew were living on one another's shoulders, this was the closest thing to paradise I could imagine.

I worked in this space for a month, and then moved on to the machine shop to take care of the tool crib. My job, so much as it was a job, consisted of issuing special tools to the machine shop personnel. The crib itself was a wire enclosure with shelves containing all the specialized tools the machinists would need to run their equipment. It was my job to get their signature on a card for any tool they requested, and then sign it off when the tool was returned. It was a good job.

The shop itself was huge. The deck heads were twenty feet high with a hatch in the center leading from the upper deck through the lower deck and down to the welding shop and foundry below. Large pieces of machinery could be lowered into either one of these spaces with one of the derricks located on the upper deck.

The machine shop itself contained just about every piece of machining apparatus you could imagine: lathes, shapers and drill presses whose sizes ranged from the very small to the absolutely enormous. To say it was impressive would be a gross understatement.

The "Cape" was the only ship on the West Coast that had a compliment of regular divers onboard: in charge P/O 1st Class "Rocky" Vassar, who I never saw dressed the entire time I was onboard, and two working divers, L/S "Smitty" Smith and A/B Ernie Maddams. I knew Ernie from when I qualified as a Clearance Diver, and I must have made an impression because they kept requesting me to work with them when they needed an extra hand on a job. Unfortunately, during working hours I couldn't be spared from the machine shop in case someone needed something from the tool crib. Not to be thwarted however, Rocky requested that the Chief Stoker change my job to Upper Deck Stoker. Under normal circumstances, on a ship that spent a lot of time at sea, this job was fairly involved, but on the Cape, where you never consumed any fuel or water, it was a fairly laid-back affair, and so I had plenty of time to work with the divers.

It was at this time, with the support of the Commanding Officer and the Chief of the Diving Unit, that I requested a transfer to the Diving Branch. What the hell, I thought. I wasn't going anywhere in this branch here.

Ottawa turned down the first of my requests. It seems they considered the fact I wore glasses a detriment, and that without them my vision would be too impaired to function optimally in a diver's environment. When it was pointed out to them that a diver's vision was always impaired underwater, they relented somewhat, so I requested the transfer again. This request was also turned down, this time the reason being that it would be a waste of public funds to transfer a man already trained as an Engineering Mechanic.

At this time, my second term was just about up, and they were trying to get me to reenlist for another 5–year stint. I decided, somewhat heatedly, that if I was such a potential waste of public funds, the powers that be could shove all my engineer's training right up their collective navy ass.

From this point on my life became a great deal more pleasant. I didn't worry about promotion or assessments, and I really started to enjoy myself on a day-to-day basis. The old Chief Stoker, thoroughly understanding my situation, more or less left me alone, and I worked with the divers the remainder of the time I was onboard. Soon thereafter we went to sea, the one and only time we did so while I was on the Cape. We sailed to Pearl Harbor and then to San Diego and for me it was like a pleasure cruise. The divers didn't do anything at sea.

I would get up in the morning, have a shower and eat breakfast, then go up to the diving locker and fool around cleaning gear for a few hours. Then at 1130 I would have my tot and anyone else's I could get my hands on, and after lunch I would have a nap before taking a tour of the ship. I was dead weight and enjoying every second of it.

When we got to Pearl it was decided we'd scrape the ship's bottom, underwater, by hand. This was no small task considering the Cape's size and all the time she'd been sitting in harbour. Her bottom was fouled up, and they estimated she was losing about two knots because of it. When you considered she could only make nine knots flat out on her best day, two was a considerable loss.

The made us up some makeshift scrapers with aluminum blades and pieces of broom handle, and every morning after breakfast we'd get suited up, head down to the small landing craft

we carried onboard with all our rigging, get in the water, and start
scraping.

Figuring the water would be too warm, we didn't wear our
wetsuits that first day, but it didn't take long to realize that with
all the energy we were using it was too cold not to. We were also
using up a lot of air. Working underwater with no place to stand,
you had to swim into the scraper to have any success, and it was
hard work.

At 1100 we'd get out of the water, have our tots, our lunch
and a little rest before getting our fresh tanks and back in the
water until 1500. Then we'd charge our tanks, shower and wash
our suits, regulator and the rest of our rigging in preparation for
the following day. This went on for two weeks, and the only
problem I had the whole time was one day after being ashore the
previous night. After having my tot and lunch, I got back in the
water and swam to the place I'd been working on before lunch,
down by the keel.

I was scraping away when I found myself getting sick, and
thinking I'd better get out of the water before this happened, started swimming the twenty-five feet along the bottom and up to the
surface. The air regulators the navy used at the time had two hoses
running from the regulator to the mouthpiece, one for the air supply and the other for the exhaust. If you took the mouthpiece out
of your mouth, you had to squeeze it in order to keep the seawater out, but some always got in anyway and you had to blow into
the mouthpiece to clear it. Still underwater, I pulled the mouthpiece from my mouth and began to vomit, and everyone knows
that when you vomit you involuntarily gasp for breath, so I took in
a good mouthful of seawater which only made things worse.
According to eyewitness accounts, I surfaced like a porpoise and lit
on the apron of the landing craft gasping for breath.

After a cup of coffee I went back into the water as good as
new, but with memories of my first dive suddenly fresh in my
head. Still, after we left Pearl Harbor they said we were making
our full nine knots, so I guess our efforts paid off.

When we got to San Diego and tied up, the British Navy hit
us up for a favour. They had a destroyer tied up in San Diego that

was heading back home from the Far East Station with a cracked A bracket, and they were wondering if we could help them. To use the Panama Canal they would need to be capable of making full power, and they wanted to get the ship to Bermuda where they had a floating dry-dock. They didn't think they could afford to have the Americans fix it, and their only other option was to steam down around South America, which was never a good idea.

We did a survey dive, and it was decided we could use Devcon, a plastic steel that worked well underwater. Splinted with sheets of stainless steel and clamps, it would give them the capability of making full power, but for how long was anyone's guess. However, according to the resident experts, it would work and it would get them through the Panama Canal.

We worked on it for two days with two-man teams, and on the third day, after I'd came out of the water, sitting on the jetty in my wetsuit alongside the ship, I saw a familiar face. "Ron Stabler!" I shouted up.

He looked down, a little puzzled.

"It's me, Mel McConaghy. We sailed together on the Britannia in '59, remember."

"McConaghy, you old rum rat. What the hell are you doing here?" he asked.

"I'm patching your ship so you can get home. Don't tell me you made Chief?"

"You bet. What about you? How are you doing?"

"I'll tell you all about it. Meet me at the gangway." After making arrangements with Rocky for one of the tenders to take my gear back to the ship and clean it up, I went aboard with Ron. We had a few tots and reminisced and agreed he'd meet me at my ship.

We met up later and had a good run ashore that night, but I came away from that episode increasingly bitter. We'd sailed together as Leading Hands, and now he was a Chief while here I was still a Leading Hand. He'd picked up three ranks while I'd picked up none. It was a bittersweet evening to be sure. I was happy to be out with an old running mate, but the thought I was getting screwed over was ever-present in my mind.

When we returned to Naden I was drafted ashore. I was assigned to the Boson's party again, but this time was a little different as I was assigned a special duty job. I was the Padre's Yeoman, which meant I cleaned up the Protestant Chapel, signed in-routines and generally killed time in the forenoon, and then changed places with the civilian secretary so I could go to the Roman Catholic Chapel and do the same thing in the afternoon. Then at 1600 I would go home. Before long I started to feel a little uncomfortable in this job where everyone seemed to be a little too concerned about my happiness. Then one day I was called up to the Regulating Office where I was told my promotion had come through, but that I'd have to sign on for another three years to get it.

"You're out of your mind if you think I'm going to sign on just to get a promotion I should've gotten three years ago," I told them. "Blackmail, I think would be a good description of this little evolution." I turned and left without being dismissed.

I spent the next three and a half months in the Release Centre, and while I kept my job almost to the end, I did undergo a few more medical examinations than expected. I was told regularly that I'd wasted a lot of my life if I was simply going to leave the navy behind at this point, but the more I was lectured on it the more I was determined to get out. On more than one occasion I was told I was stupid.

Then the day came when I walked out the main gate at Naden for the last time, in civilian clothes and with release papers in hand, wondering what life had in store for me. Over the years, I have often wondered what might have happened if I'd stayed, but in the end "what if" is a loser's game. That being said, sometimes I still miss the navy and all the good times I had, the great people I met, and the incredible places I saw, but time rolls on and so have I.

I don't regret my time in the navy. If anything, I like to think of it as a learning experience. After all, it took a shy boy from a small mill town called Aleza Lake, forty-five miles east of Prince George, and made him into a man who travelled the world eager to take on the challenges that awaited him.

ACKNOWLEDGEMENTS

I would like to acknowledge every shipmate I have ever drank a tot or ran ashore with, especially ex-RN shipmates James Sharrod and Mike Ingwood for the help they gave me navigating the world and the St. Lawrence Seaway. I was lost in the fog of age. And I would like to thank my daughter Karen, my harshest critic and toughest taskmaster, for all she has done for me, especially for keeping my ego in check.